RED HOT & SMOKIN'!

BBQ * BURGERS * BIRD

RED HOT &
SMOKIN'!

BBQ ✳ BURGERS ✳ BIRD

Basics, fundamentals
and guilty pleasures

Graeme Stockdale

NEW
HOLLAND

ACKNOWLEDGEMENTS

This book is dedicated to the memory of my good friend Gitana, and also my mother, Monica.

It was made possible by the encouragement, support and perseverance of my family – my wife Jennee and my boys Seba and Obi.

I thank my Nana Trochinski and Granny Stockdale for sparking the fire, and the man who had the knowledge, patience and skill to fuel that fire; the man I will always call 'My Chef', Paul MacNish.

I thank the team at the Stockpot Kitchen and Smokehouse BBQ, with special thanks to my sous chef Jimmy for keeping it under control while I'm typing away at this thing; and my brother Matt for always encouraging me like only a little brother can (even when he should possibly have been saying no).

I thank the peeps at New Holland Publishers and also Jody Vasallo for helping me realise this little dream I have.

Lastly, I truly thank all of my friends, family and the patrons of the Stockpot that let me feed them and live my dream of 'feeding the people'.

This book is dedicated to the memory of my good friend Gitana, and also my mother, Monica.

INTRODUCTION

Welcome comrade, to Red Hot & Smokin'! Somewhat of a food-based commentary on my not-so-very-glossy life.

The fact that this book is in your possession insinuates one of three scenarios:

- you are part of my immediate family

- you know someone in my immediate family and have stolen it from them

and/or

- you are ready to join the *foodisthebestshitever* revolution.

Whatever the reason, cooking the food you have only previously dreamt of cooking is but a lick of a finger and a flick of the page away for you now (possibly do not lick your finger if you are flicking this page on an e-book).

Use what you can find at your back door (but probably don't use your backdoor, because that would lead to half-mashed corn or carrot or similar) because that's going to be where to get your quality fresh ingredients. If you've got a local goat supplier use goat instead of lamb shoulder. If you don't like seafood, use some chicken in the chowder instead. If you don't like chili, don't eat it. I don't care.

Being flexible in the kitchen is a great thing. You come home thinking you want to make one thing, see a couple of different ingredients and decide to go off on a slight tangent, notice something else and end up making a totally different dish. I like to let the food lead me off on a journey, and in that case, a point-to-point itinerary won't suffice. I also like the food to take me out to parties, get me loaded and show me a damn good time.

And hey, my recipes are ever-changing and ever-evolving, so don't feel you have to get locked into a particular method. As I just mentioned, I certainly don't.

Oh, one final thing. Read the whole recipe before you start cooking. That way you get a gist for the whole thing and it is truly a lot harder to screw up. Let's face it, you don't want to be marooned on a deserted island, starving for something to eat and about to cook your dinner, only to realise you didn't pre-soak and cook the beans and now it's going to be hours away, do you?

OK? OK. Good luck.

This is a book with recipes in it, a recipe book if you will. Some recipes are basic and some are fundamentals that you can build on. Some take minutes, others will take a little longer to prepare. It is about quick and easy mid-week eating and, on the other side of the fence, neighbourhood-feeding table-long feasts. It is about eating well and learning to know your way around a kitchen. It is about cooking intuitively and using whatever brain you have been blessed with to its fullest capabilities!

One thing you do have to realise is this book is my interpretation, my taste and how I like things to go in general.

Use it as a guide. Try something different.

But first you'll need to bring this book to the counter and pay the nice person the required fee to take it home.

Go now child!

Wherever they are allowed to shine, condiments will steal your heart.

CHAPTER 1

Condiments

CON·DI·MENT / 'KND-MNT / *NOUN*

A substance, such as a relish, vinegar, or spice,
used to flavor or complement food.
[Middle English, from Old French, from Latin
condmentum, from *condre*, to season.]

CONDIMENTS WITH BREAKFAST. Condiments with lunch. Condiments with dinner. Condiments for three days worth of leftover meats after no one showed up to your annual gerbil appreciation society barbecue. Wherever they are allowed to shine, condiments will steal your heart.

Too often condiments are disregarded, second-class citizens, relegated to the back of a cookbook (or even worse: the masterfoods section of the local supermarket), and not even given the respect of having a little picture all of their own. Well, it's **TIME TO BRING THESE UNSUNG HEROES OUT** of the shadows and into the limelight. Condiments, your time has come.

Who on earth opens their book with a chapter about condiments? Me. I open my book with a chapter on condiments. Clearly.

Condiments are the only thing needed to bring a piece of perfectly cooked meat to the glorious heights of the agenda of the local P&C or CWA monthly meeting. If the meat is the beach, then the condiment is the pretty girl sunbathing on it. If the meat is the little pink unicorn, the condiment is the golden horn. If the meat is your hangover, the condiment is your aspirin dissolved in a bloody Mary. You're getting the picture now, yeah?

It is not a culinary mystery what a good sauce or dressing will do to bring a meal together. You will not see that scrawled across the front page of the local paper, or on next Thursday's episode of CSI:Miami, but I kid you not, smart people have been doing it for years.

My life of culinary adventure is granted the freedom to roam upon whichever fields of distant lands it wishes – by the use of condiments. Just the smell of fish sauce, lime juice and coriander can take you to the markets of South East Asia, pulled pork with Carolina mustard sauce will have you dreaming of a whole hog hoedown in the American South, while a good rib-eye steak with chimichurri is going to take you straight to the farmlands of Argentina. No, the addition of a condiment is not the same as creating a traditional ethnic dish, but a little escapism for time to time sure is nice, isn't it?! What is a better form of escapism than food? Even if a meal takes you to a lovely little place you have made up all by yourself, that meal is a damn fine meal indeed and you, my friend, have now evolved from the days of a hairy primate living in a tree, eating only because you need to, into a fully fledged lover of food; even, if I may, a person who has realized the full potential of **SOME CRACKING GOOD CONDIMENTS.**

This chapter contains a few of my most used favorites, but throughout the book there will be numerous extra condiments for you to play with as you will.

Now you should pat yourself on the back while I gather my thoughts and get moving on a couple of recipes for you ...

MAYONNAISE

I'll start with one of my all time favorite condiments. Mayonnaise. It's highly versatile and a damn good friend in your time of need.

If you're not scared about making an emulsified dressing for the first time … you should be. You should be. Not that I'm concerned. You're going to do just fine.

The first and foremost rule of your first emulsification (and many other firsts in life I may add) is GO SLOWLY. This is not a race. Unless of course you are in a mayonnaise-making race, in which case you should go really fast. The hopes of your country are riding on you right now. Whisk, whisk, whisk!

Once you know how to make mayonnaise, a whole world of condiments will be at your fingertips … aioli, tartare and flavored mayos as varied as your mind can imagine. Here, let me be of assistance with some suggested additions: seeded mustard, smoked paprika, saffron, charred chili … anything.

Basic Mayo

2 egg yolks

1 tsp (¼ fl oz) Dijon mustard

1 tbsp (fl oz) apple cider vinegar or lemon juice (or something else acidic)

250 ml (8 fl oz) vegetable oil

A splash of water if it needs thinning out

Salt and pepper

Put the egg yolks, mustard, vinegar and a pinch of salt and pepper into a bowl if you are hand whisking this, or into a round tub if you live in a country that has electricity and you have the common sense to own a stick mixer.

Whisk until the yolks start to fluff up and turn pale.

While whisking, slowly add the oil in a light trickle. Don't stop whisking while you're doing this.

You should notice that it is all binding together into one glorious spreadable mass. Do not be tempted to pour the oil in quickly. Take it nice and slow.

Once all of the oil is in there add a drop or two of water to get it to your desired consistency, and check seasoning. Always check in with the seasoning.

If this is your first time, smear some of your finished mayo on a piece of fresh bread and taste the results. Mmmmm …

Remaining mayonnaise will last covered in the refrigerator for 2—3 days.

Aioli

Aioli is as simple as adding 1-2 cloves of garlic (minced) to the egg mix of your mayonnaise (recipe Page 14) before you start emulsifying the oil into it. Bam.

RANCH DRESSING

250 ml (8 fl oz) mayonnaise

175 ml (6 fl oz) buttermilk

60 ml (2 fl oz) cup sour cream

¼ small onion, minced

1 clove garlic, minced

1 pinch dried thyme

1 tbsp finely chopped parsley

Salt and pepper

All ingredients go into a large mixing bowl (or your partners' cupped hands could possibly do the same job). Mix it up. Heaps easy.

Dill Ranch Dressing

Simply take the recipe for ranch dressing (above), only substitute 1 tablespoon of chopped fresh dill for the dried thyme.

TOMATO KETCHUP

The thing that should be noted right now is the fact that this chapter is really all about the tomato sauce/ketchup. I have been working on perfecting this condiment for a few years now — just like my belly, and my ability to amuse passers-by with my boyish wit and charm.

Seriously though, homemade tomato sauce has been perplexing me for years. It had an actual Grazza proof hex on it that prevented me from ever knowing its ways. The recipe for tomato sauce was hidden from my eyes, deep within a chest buried on a deserted island, where I would never be able to find it … until now. That's right. I have cracked my seven-year itch and now have the ability to make top-notch tomato sauce. In your face seven-year itch! And heed these words that are shared with you, via my finger, the keys on my laptop and this book; it is not a recipe that is easy for me to give up — but no use taking the thing to the grave with me. It's not like I have a cute little white goatee, Colonel status and a penchant for fried chicken. Although I do think it's very clear that I enjoy good fried chicken.

So here we go, and if you think it looks like it has a lot of sugar in it, that's because it does.

Three cups of that sweet, sweet shimmering goodness to one and a half kilos of tomatoes ... plus it has maple syrup too.

Ooh la la!

Season with salt and pepper.

Bottle up for your next hamburger, BBQ or cheese sandwich. It will last sealed in the refrigerator for 1 month.

CAROLINA MUSTARD SAUCE

1.5 kg (3 ½ lb) ripe tomatoes (the same amount of tomato passata will do the trick)

250 g (9 oz) tomato paste

1 brown onion, diced

6 cloves garlic, peeled and crushed

2 cloves

A splash of hot sauce

600 g (21 oz) caster sugar

60 ml (2 fl oz) maple syrup

250 ml (8 fl oz) white wine vinegar

Salt and pepper

Soften the onions and garlic in a little oil.

Add everything else and simmer slowly for an hour.

Blitz and pass through a sieve, or just blitz really well ... I don't like chunky bits in my tomato sauce.

Check viscosity by placing a tablespoon of sauce into the fridge to set. A few minutes should do the trick.

If it needs to be a little thicker return to heat until desired consistency is achieved.

175 ml (6 fl oz) American-style mustard

175 ml (6 fl oz) apple cider vinegar

1 tbsp light brown sugar

2 tbsp Worcestershire sauce

2 tsp hot sauce (optional, if you want some spice)

2 tsp salt

1 tsp ground black pepper

Combine all ingredients in a bowl and whisk to combine.

Store remainder. In a sealed container in the fridge this should keep for ages – at least a few months (though I have never needed to test this theory in my household!).

APPLE CIDER VINAIGRETTE

250 ml (8 fl oz) American-style mustard

150 g (5 oz) caster sugar

400 ml (13 fl oz) apple cider vinegar

1200 ml (2 pint) vegetable oil

Salt and pepper

Pour mustard, sugar and apple cider vinegar into a large mixing bowl if you are hand whisking, or a food processor if not.

Slowly emulsify oils into other ingredients by adding gradually while you mix (as with mayonnaise page 14).

Season with salt and pepper.

This dressing will last indefinitely in the refrigerator.

BBQ SAUCE

625 ml (1 pint) tomato paste

700 g (25 oz) brown sugar

500 (16 fl oz) ml maple syrup

250 ml (8 fl oz) apple cider vinegar

4 tbsp smoked paprika

1 ½ tbsp onion powder

1 ½ tbsp garlic powder

1 ½ tbsp ground cumin

¾ tbsp dried chili flakes

¾ tbsp black pepper

1 ½ tbsp salt

75–100 g (3–3 ½ oz) cornflour (corn starch)

2 ½ l (4 pint) water

In a large, heavy-based pot, add all the ingredients except the cornflour and water and cook out over low heat for 15 minutes, stirring often.

Make a slurry* out of the cornflour and 2 cups of water. Set aside.

Add remaining water to the pot and mix thoroughly until fully combined. Simmer for 30 minutes, stirring often.

Whisk in most of the cornflour slurry and simmer for another 2 minutes.

Remove from heat. Place 2 tablespoons of sauce into a small bowl and place in the fridge for a few minutes to cool down. This is going to give you an accurate measure of viscosity.

If the sauce needs to be a little thicker for your liking, return it to heat, whisk in the remaining cornflour slurry and simmer for another 2 minutes.

Bam. You're all over this condiment business now.

Store BBQ sauce in a sealed container in the fridge for up to a month.

*A slurry is a combination of starch and cold water which is then added to hot preparations as a thickener. Common starches are corn starch or corn flour, flour, potato starch or arrowroot.

SPICY BALLS BBQ SAUCE

1 L (32 fl oz) BBQ sauce (page 17)

250 ml (8 fl oz) tinned chipotle in adobo

Combine in a blender or blitz with a stick whizz until smooth.

Store BBQ sauce in a sealed container in the fridge for up to a month.

THE BIG RED RUB

Contrary to what you may initially believe, this does not involve a visit from a burly Scottish highlander who has just completed an online course in the fine art of exotic massage. This is a dry rub for meats that is both red in color and big in flavor. I am also the creator of the Big Red Rub and throughout these hills and haystacks, I am oft-known by the name Big Red ... so you could quite possibly see how I think I am being heaps clever.

This is my go-to rub for pork and chicken cooked with flame or fryer, and you will find it used frequently in other recipes in this book.

Depending on how much you want, a 'part' can be a tablespoon, a cup, or even an old moonshine jar. It's totally up to you.

4 parts sweet paprika

1 part brown sugar

1 part salt

1 part onion powder

1 part garlic powder

1 part ground cumin

1 part ground chili

1 part dried oregano

1 part dried thyme

Mix it all together in a large bowl, and you're good to go.

Make heaps and give it to your friends, or store in an airtight container in the cupboard for up to a month.

BIG RED Rub

CHIMICHURRI

I do have a penchant for fresh herby dressings and the good thing about this one is that it has the extra kick of a bit of chili to weed out the men from the boys. This steak sauce originated in Argentina, but now it is destined for my belly (and perhaps yours?).

2 cups loosely packed oregano

2 cups loosely packed parsley

3 long red chilis, seeds in if you like it hot, chopped roughly

3—4 cloves garlic, chopped roughly

30 ml (1 fl oz) red wine vinegar

250 ml (8 fl oz) olive oil

Salt

Put everything except oil into a food processor or blender. Blitz and add oil slowly.

Check the seasoning and adjust if necessary.

This will last for a few days in a sealed container in the fridge, no problems.

BIG RED HOT SAUCE

This stuff is on the table with every, I repeat, every meal we have.

1 kg (2 ¼ lb) long red chilis*

2 cloves garlic, peeled

100 g (3 ½ oz) caster sugar

1 tbsp salt

250ml (8 fl oz) white vinegar

500ml (16 fl oz) water

Blitz or chop the chili and garlic to a rough consistency.

Transfer to a glass jar and add all other ingredients. Sit on the kitchen bench for a week, stirring every day.

Transfer chili mixture to a pot and heat the sauce until it comes to a simmer. Simmer for 10 minutes, stirring every now and then.

Allow to cool and then puree to a smooth consistency with a stick wizz or in a blender.

Seal and store in the refrigerator.

Hot sauce will keep for ... actually I don't know how long because it's always gone within a month around these parts. You'll be safe keeping it for a month or so in a sealed container in the fridge.

*To be quite frank with you, I have used just about every chili you could imagine. All of them work. It just depends what the word 'hot' means to you. I know for a fact that to some people hot means the tiniest little flick of a very mild chili into their curry, while others will splash about the hottest-of-the-hot chili hot sauce until they are bleeding from their eyes.

ZA'ATAR

This is one of my favorite little spice blends. Apparently it's pretty big in the Middle East too.

It's exceptionally good at being that little something you have in the cupboard for when you just need to sprinkle some deliciousness on your food.

You can sprinkle this stuff on everything:

- roasted vegetables
- salad
- chicken
- fish
- lamb
- labne
- olives
- soft cheese
- fries or cold chips/crisps

You can sprinkle it on flat bread with a little splash of olive oil and then toast it to make your own crisp bread for scooping up olives and hummus and so on, in a mezze-style platter, or you can just sprinkle it straight onto your hummus or baba ganoush to enhance your dip.

You can make an awesome Middle Eastern pizza with lamb mince, onion and good sprinkling of za'atar. It's always a great addition.

2 tbsp dried thyme

2 tbsp sumac

2 tsp dried oregano

2 tsp dried marjoram

125 ml (4 fl oz) sesame seeds, lightly toasted

1 tsp salt

Pulse all ingredients in a food processor until it's a little broken up. For a chunkier za'atar, instead of a food processor simply put all ingredients in a plastic container or jar, seal and shake to combine.

Za'atar will last for 2 weeks.

Try messing with the quantities or using different combinations of herbs to create your very own version of za'atar.

KIMCHI

(For the refrigerator)

Kimchi is a fiery looking, fermented chili cabbage condiment. *Seriously* fiery looking, which shouldn't put you off using it liberally.

Important note: kimchi is incredibly addictive. My love for kimchi has found me cooking plain steamed rice for dinner, so I can eat it with a fat pile of kimchi. This is not an exaggeration … I have often enjoyed a toasted cheese and kimchi sandwich, or even taken it one step further to create the karaage fried chicken, kimchi and Japanese mayo toasted sandwich deluxe. I have also made cucumber kimchi, which has found me cooking burgers so it may have a friend on its way to my belly, or simply eating it on its own. Cucumber kimchi is also very addictive.

Just one more thing to note about kimchi is, as with all fermented cabbage products, it is really good for digestion.

Go now child. Try it.

1 wombok (Chinese cabbage)

50 g (2 oz) salt

1 tbsp caster sugar

125 ml (4 fl oz) fish sauce

10 cloves garlic, peeled and crushed

½ thumb-sized knob ginger, chopped

½ brown onion, chopped

50 g (2 oz) dried chili flakes, soaked

in enough hot water to cover

Quarter the cabbages through the length and then cut it into 5cm pieces, discarding the core.

Place the cabbage in a large, clean bucket or tub and fill with enough water to cover. Add salt and give it a good mix.

Leave the cabbage to soak for 4–5 hours, turning every hour. Rinse and drain cabbage.

Add all other ingredients to a food processor or blender and blitz into a coarse paste.

Spread the mix over the cabbage and return to the clean tub. Seal and store on the bench for 2 days until it starts to ferment. It will start to bubble a little bit and the smell will intensify.

Whack it into sterilised jars or plastic containers and store it in the fridge to halt the fermentation.

It is ready to be eaten straight away, but I like it best after a few days in the fridge so all of the flavors can truly get to know each other and really develop lasting friendships.

This stuff will last in the fridge for a month or two, but good luck not eating it all before then.

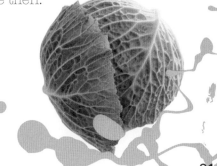

SAUERKRAUT

(For the refrigerator)

1 large green cabbage

1 ½ tbsp sea salt

1 tsp caraway seeds

Quarter the cabbage through the core and slice it nice and fine. A mandoline is great for this.

Transfer the cabbage to a large mixing bowl and sprinkle the salt over. Chuck the caraway seeds in now, too. Work the salt into the cabbage and then let it sit for an hour or so, to draw out the moisture.

Grab handfuls of the cabbage and pack them a large (clean) jar or even a bucket. Every so often, squash down the cabbage in the jar with your fist.

Once all the cabbage is packed into the jar, slip a smaller jar or ramekin into the mouth of the jar and weigh it down with a tin of something. This will help keep the cabbage weighed down, and eventually, submerged beneath its liquid.

Cover the mouth of the jar with a cloth for air flow and insect protection.

Over the next 24 hours press down on the cabbage every so often with the smaller jar. As the cabbage releases its liquid, it will become more limp and compact and the liquid will rise over the top of the cabbage.

After 24 hours, if the liquid has not risen above the cabbage, dissolve 1 teaspoon of salt in 1 cup of water and add enough to submerge the cabbage.

Let the cabbage ferment on the bench top for 2—5 days (it will ferment faster in warmer climates).

Store covered in the refrigerator.

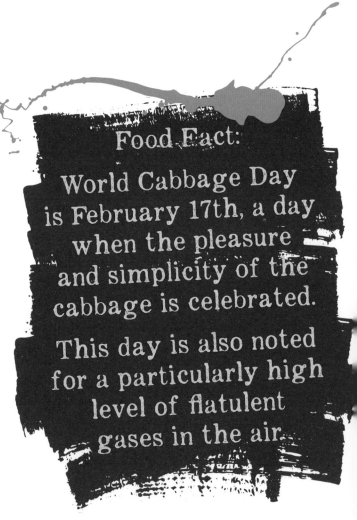

Food Fact:

World Cabbage Day is February 17th, a day when the pleasure and simplicity of the cabbage is celebrated.

This day is also noted for a particularly high level of flatulent gases in the air.

Have a go - a great compliment with meals!

International Fried Chicken Day!

CHAPTER 2

Fried chicken

(& Things to go with it)

This recipe was created on international fried chicken day. Just the fact that there is an international fried chicken day was enough to get me going on this.

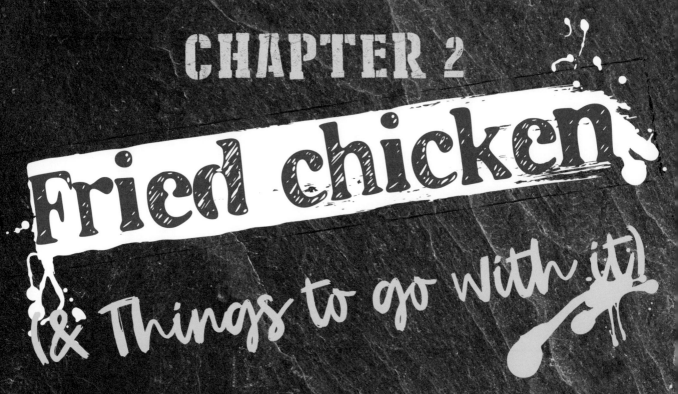

This was one of those meals that morphed a little mid-prep. It didn't do a full Dr Jekyll and Mr Hyde, but it did change its original guise ever so slightly.

On this day I declared mid-shift that I had a hankering for some fried chicken. When it came time to prepare the family meal for the evening, fried chicken would indeed be what I would concoct and in turn consume – karaage style. I cut the chicken thigh, I pulled the potato flour from its home on the flour shelf, I got that chicken chopped up ... and then I stopped. I reversed that old pick-up truck back to the fork in the road, crunched the gear-box back into first and then floored it heading down the other track.

This is where I stopped making karaage chicken.

I mixed some patented Big Red Rub (page 18) in with the chicken, cracked an egg in there to really give the flour something to stick to, thoroughly dusted the chicken pieces and then fried them up.

Real good.
Proper good.

The chicken was consumed with crinkle cut potato chips from the freezer section, a what-we-had-in-the-fridge salad, homemade mayonnaise (page 14) and hot sauce (page 19).

The kids were really, really happy with this and it was cheap and relatively easy to make, so I guess you should just go and make it. Do it for the kids.

That was a few years back and the start of what I would definitely call my 'fried chicken phase', before it got all trendy.

Since then I have experimented. A lot. I have created a fried chicken recipe that is gluten and dairy free (no buttermilk, no lactic acid) to suit these dietary requirements. I have learnt that if I marinate the chicken for 12 hours it really does inject it with a heap more flavor and also a little extra moistness. So that's why I do it like I do it.

You're going to need a deep fryer, large pot or cauldron suitable for deep frying. Also, for deep frying I use canola oil or something similar – just no olive oil!

Fried Chicken & sides

BIG RED RUB

REALLY GOOD FRIED CHICKEN

(Serves 4-6; begin this recipe a day ahead)

1 whole free-range bird* or 6 chicken marylands, separated into legs and thighs

2 eggs, beaten

300 g (10 ½ oz) potato flour

150 g (5 oz) Big Red Rub (page 18)

Oil to deep fry

Marinate the chicken in the Big Red Rub overnight.

Roll the chicken through the egg mix and then the potato flour.

Give the chicken a little tap to remove excess flour. Just a little love tap though – don't get carried away and end up giving your chicken a full blown spanking.

Heat your oil in your deep fryer to 160°C (325°F).

Now fry the chicken in batches. Four or five pieces at a time is probably good, for 16 minutes per batch (if you have a thermometer you can check the internal temperature in the thickest part of the chicken – it should be 75 C (165 F)), keeping each batch warm in a low oven until they're all done.

Season with Big Red seasoning (page 29) and serve. I hope your Chicken Gravy (page 30) is ready!

*If you can, joint (a fancy word for 'break') this bird into **8** pieces. If you don't have the skills to do this yourself, ask your butcher very politely if he/she will do it.

Please be sure to use your manners.

BIG RED SEASONING MIX

2 parts Big Red Rub (page 18)

1 part salt

Grind this mix up super fine in a spice grinder and sprinkle it over everything, from fried or roast chicken, to pork or sausages, to tempura vegetables, chips or potato wedges.

Store seasoning in an airtight container for up to 1 month.

Food Facts:

Fresh chilies will be spicier during the summer period and milder in the cooler months.

Apparently elephants can't stand the smell of chili. So a pocket full of chili would be very handy if you were getting run down by a herd of stampeding elephants.

CHICKEN GRAVY

2 kg (4 ½ lb) chicken carcasses or wings

2 brown onions, quartered (you can leave the skin on if you want. I'll let you in on a little secret; I always leave the skin on my vegetables when I make stock)

2 carrots, roughly chopped

2 sticks celery, roughly chopped

1 bulb garlic, sliced through the middle

5 sprigs thyme

Salt and white pepper

50 g (2 oz) plain flour (or cornflour/corn starch for gluten free)

Place all ingredients except cornflour into a baking dish and roast at 220°C (350–430°F) for 30 minutes or until properly browned.

Once browned, get everything into a pot, making sure to scrape all of the little crusty bits from the bottom of the pan in there too. Cover with water and simmer over medium heat for 3 hours. If your stock is now smelling like Nanna's chicken soup you are ready to make your gravy.

Strain your stock through a chinois or large sieve into another pot, and return to medium heat. Reduce to 1 L.

Make a slurry out of the cornflour and ½ a cup of water.

Whisking constantly, slowly add ¾ of the flour slurry to the stock, reserving a little to adjust thickness if necessary.

Continue to simmer and stir gravy for 2–3 minutes to cook out the flour.

Check the viscosity. If it is a little thick you can whisk in a splash of water to thin it out. If it is a little thin you can whisk in the remaining slurry and cook it out for another couple of minutes.

'SLAW

It seems to me, via Wikipedia, that the Dutch first penned a recipe for modern day coleslaw in the late 1700s (coleslaw derived from the Dutch koolsla; kool meaning cabbage and sla meaning salad). There is also reference to the Germans and Polish for their contribution. This actually came as a bit of a surprise to me as I was sure it would've been an All American Barbeque recipe, created by the Yanks. Upon further thought I decided it makes a lot of sense that this was possibly the product of a German-Polish coalition, as that is quite literally how I made my way into existence, and hence would explain the love I have for this shredded cabbage salad.

I don't even think love is a strapping enough word. Love is the word one uses when describing their feelings for their life partner, their children, or possibly their favorite flavor at the local ice cream parlor. I think the word that I need to be using is *addicted*. I am addicted to the consumption of coleslaw with every part of my being. I don't care what season it is, how cold it is or who is coming for dinner, there is always a place at my dinner table for coleslaw – there may not be enough space for you, but coleslaw can wander in anytime. There is a little plaque on my table with 'coleslaw' engraved on it, much like what you would see on the parking space of a company executive. There's no way the potato salad or tabbouleh is going to get to sit there, just on the off chance the coleslaw might show up!

A mandoline is great to make short work of shredding cabbage and slicing things nice and thin. It has also been known in its time to scalp the fingertip of the over-confident user.

I shall call this my honky dory 'slaw. It has cabbage and a bit of carrot in it, which I feel is a solid start. It's dressed with a mix of

Apple Cider Vinaigrette for a little tarty sweetness and homemade Mayonnaise for its mayonnaisiness ... Delicious. Japanese mayonnaise would do the job too.

'Yup. German and Polish grandparents. Made their way over here after the war. They were pretty happy with their decision, as am I.

Honky Dory Coleslaw

(Serves 6 as a side)

½ a medium green cabbage, finely shredded

1 carrot, grated

125 ml (4 fl oz) Apple Cider Vinaigrette (page 17)

125 ml (4 fl oz) Mayonnaise (page 14)

Combine all ingredients in a large bowl and mix well.

Check and adjust seasoning if necessary.

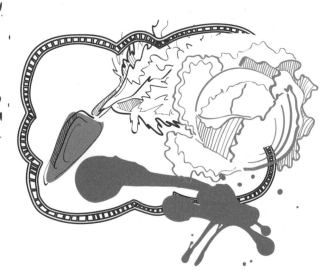

Healthy options!

Healthy options!

Kale & Apple 'Slaw

(Serves 6 as a side)

This recipe is for when you want to be a little more fancy, or healthy.

¼ green cabbage, finely shredded

¼ red cabbage, finely shredded

4-5 leaves of curly kale (the kind the hippies love), finely shredded

2 green apples, finely shredded (be sure to shred the apples just before serving or they will oxidise and turn brown)

250 ml (8 fl oz) Apple Cider Vinaigrette (page 17)

Combine all salad ingredients and dress lightly, or however you want. It is your salad, after all.

DEEP FRIED POTATO CHIPS

(Serves 6 as a side)

5—6 medium potatoes, skin on (Sebago is my choice), washed if needed, cut into 1 cm chips

Salt and pepper

Fill deep fryer with oil to level.

Get oil up to temperature. Around 180°C (350°F) is good.

In batches, blanch chips in oil for 2 minutes. Allow oil to come back to correct temperature between each batch.

Repeat step 2.

Now they go in for the final time, 2 minutes should do the trick. They should be golden brown and crispy.

Season and serve.

OVEN CHIPS

(Serves 6 as a side)

5—6 medium potatoes skin on (Sebago is my choice), washed if needed, cut into 1cm chips

Salt and pepper

Blanch potatoes in boiling water for 2—3 minutes. This makes them better, trust me. Strain them and allow to cool.

Spread out on an oven tray, splash with however much oil your diet will allow and season generously.

Bake at 200°C (400°F) for 25 minutes, tossing regularly.

Now they should be golden brown and crispy.

Season and serve.

HEALTHY ALTERNATIVE!

MASHED POTATO

(Serves 6 as a side)

1 kg (2 ¼ lb) Dutch cream potatoes, peeled and cut into large dice

250 g (9 oz) butter, chopped into large dice

250–300 ml (8–10 fl oz) full cream milk

Salt

Boil or steam the potatoes until they are cooked. Strain and leave to dry out for five minutes. This will help extra moisture to evaporate and make your potatoes hungry for butter.

Mash potatoes using a ricer* if you have one, or old-school style with your potato masher.

Stir through butter until it is all fully absorbed by your hungry potatoes.

Stir through milk until your desired consistency is reached.

Season with a good hit of salt. Potatoes love salt. They will probably grow up and get married one day, but for now we're happy seeing their love flourish in a bowl of mashed potato on our dinner table.

*A ricer, also known as a potato ricer, is a bit like a garlic crusher, but potato sized; basically it is used to process potatoes (and other foods) by forcing it through small steel holes about the size of a grain of rice.

JENNEE'S CORN BREAD

(For the table, plus leftovers for tomorrow)

We sell a lot of this stuff at the restaurant. That must mean it's at least a bit good, right?

75 g (3 oz) raw sugar

3 eggs

375g (13 oz) self-raising flour

250g (8 ½ oz) polenta

1 tsp salt

2 tbsp baking powder

280 ml (9 fl oz) full cream milk

280 ml (9 fl oz) buttermilk

60 ml (2 fl oz) vegetable oil

110 g (4 oz) butter, softened

Sea salt, to garnish

Smoked paprika, to garnish

Preheat oven to 180°C (350°F).

In a cake mixer, whisk eggs and sugar until pale.

Add butter and oil, whisk until combined.

Add milks and whisk until combined.

Add polenta and whisk until combined.

Finally, add flour, baking powder and salt. Whisk well for 10 minutes, scraping sides regularly.

Jennee's corn bread

Jennee's corn bread salad

Pour into a large lined cake tin and sprinkle lightly with coarse salt and smoked paprika.

Bake in preheated oven, rotating every 10 minutes.

Cook until golden. If it looks like it's getting too brown then reduce temperature to 150°C (300°F) for last 10–20 minutes.

Total baking time should be about an hour.

We put this on the table with smoked honey butter and people like it a lot.

TATER TOTS

(Serves 6 as a side)

1 kg (2 ¼ lb) Desiree or Dutch cream potatoes

Salt and pepper

Boil potatoes whole and with their skin on for ten minutes (bear with me here). The potatoes will now be slightly cooked.

Let the potatoes cool a little and then coarsely grate. Season grated potato with salt and pepper.

Form potato into little tater tot nuggets by squeezing a spoonful of mix at the base of your thumb and finger on one hand and compacting with the thumb and finger of your other hand.

Deep fry in batches for 3–4 minutes until golden brown.

Season with salt, serve with Aioli (page 15) and Hot Sauce (page 19).

SPICY CHICKEN FINGERS

If you have a good butcher you might be able to get hold of a little treat known as the chicken finger. There are two of these per bird, located above the back bone where it joins to the wing, so basically treat them like gold.

If you cannot get hold of the chicken finger, fear not, as the chicken wing segment is also a very fitting substitute.

These tasty little morsels ask for the exact same cooking method as the full sized chicken but require only 4–5 minutes cooking time. I then season them with Big Red Seasoning (page 29), toss them through a healthy dose of hot sauce (page 19) and then serve them with a few pickles (page 56) and Alabama White BBQ Sauce (page 44).

ALABAMA WHITE BBQ SAUCE

AKA my lord white sauce.

250 ml (8 fl oz) mayonnaise (page 14)

80 ml (3 fl oz) apple cider vinegar (page 17)

1 tsp sugar

1 tsp garlic powder

A pinch or so cayenne powder

Salt and pepper

Combine all ingredients in a bowl and mix thoroughly.

Seal and store in the refrigerator for up to 1 week.

CRUNCHY FRIDGE SALAD

A pretty simple recipe that you can put your own spin on with the ingredients.

A handful or so of:

snow peas, julienned

green beans, cut in half

Granny Smith apple, julienned

cabbage, shredded

iceberg lettuce, shredded

sprouts

fennel, sliced

radish, sliced

A few torn mint leaves

A good splash of Apple Cider Vinaigrette (page 17), to dress.

Get it all into a large mixing bowl.

Mix it all together.

Pretty simple, eh?!

BEER BATTERED ONION RINGS

(This recipe is enough for a few sides or maybe a Friday night on the couch)

2 large onions of your choosing

125 g (4 ½ oz) plain flour, plus extra to dust

150 g (5 oz) self-raising flour

1 tbsp oil

1 tbsp Big Red Rub (page 18)

1 bottle of beer – whatever you're drinking will be fine

Ranch Dressing (page 15) and Big Red Seasoning (page 29) to serve

Slice onions into 1 cm (½ inch) rings; pop out the first 4-5 center rings and set aside for something else, keeping the large outer rings.

Heat oil in a deep fryer or pot, to 180°C (350°F).

To make the batter, mix flours, oil and

Friday night on the couch ...

Southern Fried

spice mix. Slowly whisk in the beer until your batter is quite smooth and is thick enough to coat your finger nicely. Not too thick is the key here.

Coat the onion rings with plain flour and then dip them into the batter. Drag them out of the batter and ever-so-slightly drag them across the side of the bowl to remove excess batter.

Lower them gently into the oil and fry for 2–3 minutes until crisp and golden, turning half way through.

Drain on kitchen towel, season with Big Red seasoning and serve with ranch sauce on the side.

BARRAMUNDI WINGS SOUTHERN FRIED

(Serves 4)

Fish wings are the tasty little triangle of meat cut from between the fish's gill and stomach (not totally dissimilar to a chicken wing in appearance (except for the fin. And the scales. Okay, they are a little bit dissimilar), and often used for bait in crab traps or something of the like. Your fish monger should know what you're talking about.

These tasty little morsels will have you coming back time and time again. This is a fish meal that will give you good bang for your buck, as all of the ingredients cost next to nothing but the result is still damn well delicious.

There is nothing about this dish that isn't to be loved: the price, the taste, the sustainability … I love it more than my arm. Not my right arm of course, but I could do without lefty if it came down to the choice between him and the fish wings. Sorry lefty, I really am.

These things came up even better than expected. Some homemade hot sauce and ranch dressing to complete the package and I was ready to pat myself on the back, get comfy, whisper a few sweet nothings into my own ear and check which arm I still had attached.

1 ½ kg (3 ¼ lb) fish wings (12 wings), scaled

2 eggs, whisked

150 g (5 oz) Big Red Rub (page 18) or your favorite Southern/Creole/ Cajun seasoning

250 g (9 oz) potato flour (starch)

Salt

Start heating some oil for deep frying. 180°C (350°F) is a pretty good temp for this little project.

While oil is heating, combine fish wings and red seasoning in a large bowl and toss to coat.

Add eggs and mix to coat.

Dredge wings through potato flour and toss to coat. Rubber gloves can be handy here if you don't like getting all icky and sticky. You want the wings to be quite dry coated, not a wet batter, so if you need to add a little extra potato flour, you do that right now.

Once the oil is up to temperature, give the wings a little tap to get rid of any extra flour and drop them gently into the oil. 5 minutes is pretty much bang on for a medium sized fish wing.

Once cooked, remove them from the oil, drain in a basket or on absorbent paper, season with salt and serve drizzled with Hot Sauce (page 19) and Ranch Dressing (page 15), and with a nice coleslaw (page 32) on the side.

PULLED PORK & MUSTARD SPRING ROLLS

WITH BBQ SAUCE

(Makes 12 spring rolls)

This is a cracking way to use up leftover pulled pork, or you can use brisket, smoked chicken, or whatever you have to hand.

Spring roll wrappers should be available in the freezer section of your local Asian supermarket, or even a lot of the big chain stores these days.

1 kg (2 ¼ lb) pulled pork (page 95)

¼ small cabbage, shredded to make roughly the same volume as the pork

1 carrot, grated

2 tbsp American-style mustard

Salt and pepper

12 spring roll wrappers

BBQ sauce (page 17), to serve

Big Red Seasoning (page 29), to serve

Start heating oil for deep frying, to 180°C (350°F).

Meanwhile, combine all ingredients except spring roll wrappers in a large mixing bowl, and mix gently to combine.

Fusion? ...

Great party snack!

50

Check seasoning and adjust if necessary.

Portion onto 12 spring roll wrappers and roll. There are plenty of helpful tutorials online where you can learn rolling techniques.

Deep fry at 180°C (350°F) for 3—4 minutes, until golden brown.

Serve, dusted with Big Red Seasoning and with BBQ sauce on the side.

Heat deep fryer oil to 160°C (300°F).

Scoop dessert spoon sized fritters into hot oil.

Fry for 3—4 minutes until golden brown and cooked through.

Drain on absorbent paper, transfer to oven tray and keep warm in a low oven until all hush puppies are cooked.

Season with salt and pepper and serve with something to dip them in – aioli, sour cream, hot sauce, the world is your oyster.

HUSH PUPPIES

(serves a few as a party snack)

Dry ingredients

400 g (14 oz) polenta

125 g (4 ½ oz) self-raising flour

½ tbsp smoked paprika

½ tbsp sugar

½ tbsp salt

1 brown onion, diced

200 g (7 oz) grated cheddar cheese

2 pickled jalapeños, chopped

A handful of chopped parsley

Wet ingredients

375 ml (12 fl oz) milk

3 eggs

Salt and pepper

Mix dry and wet ingredients separately.

Combine and stir through until just together.

HOMINY CHEESE BAKE

(For the table)

2x 400g (14 oz) tins of hominy*, strained

1 brown onion, diced

125 g (4 ½ oz) grated cheddar cheese

125 g (4 ½ oz) Monterey Jack cheese, or other cheese

½ green chili, chopped

125 ml (4 fl oz) sour cream

1 tsp smoked paprika

Salt

200 g fresh breadcrumbs

Add a splash of oil to a medium-hot pan and sauté onions and chili until slightly browned.

Add hominy and heat through.

Combine all except breadcrumbs and check seasoning.

Pour into a baking dish, top with breadcrumbs and bake in 180°C (350°F) oven for 30–40 minutes until golden brown and bubbling.

Food Fact:
*Hominy, if you don't know, is dried maize (corn) kernels that have been treated with an alkaline solution.

TRUFFLE MAC 'N' CHEESE

(For the table)

250 g (9 oz) macaroni, cooked per packet instructions

400 g (14 oz) grated cheddar cheese

150 g (5 oz) grated Parmesan

250 ml (8 fl oz) cream

750ml (24 fl oz) loose béchamel sauce (see method below)

1 ½ tbsp truffle paste

1 tbsp hot sauce

Salt and pepper

Crushed cheese flavored corn chips, to serve

For the béchamel sauce:

3 tbsp butter

3 tbsp plain flour

750ml (24 fl oz) milk

Salt a nd pepper

Gently melt butter in a pot over medium heat.

Add flour and cook out for a minute, stirring constantly, so flour does not burn.

Add milk, roughly half a cup at a time, and whisk to ensure a smooth consistency.

Once all milk is added cook out for another minute or two, whisking often.

Season with a little salt and pepper and it is good to go.

Gently heat your béchamel sauce in a pot over medium heat.

Add all ingredients except macaroni. Stir to combine and melt cheese.

Heat pasta by quickly dipping into a pot of boiling water and then straining.

Add macaroni to sauce and stir to combine.

Check seasoning and adjust if necessary.

Top with crushed corn chips and serve.

If you have some leftovers the next day, feel free to slice it into squares, crumb it up and deep fry them for Tasty Fried Mac 'n' Cheese Bites.

SEXY CORN

(CORN ON THE COB WITH MAY-ONNAISE, PECORINO & HERBS)

(For the table)

4 ears of sweet corn, husks removed, cut in half

50 g (2 oz) pecorino, finely grated with a microplane

½ tsp dried ancho chili flakes

1 large handful mixed fresh herbs – for example, parsley, coriander, oregano and thyme – chopped

125 ml (4 fl oz) mayonnaise

1 lime, quartered, to serve

Boil or grill corn until just cooked, 5 minutes should do the trick.

Mix cheese, chili and herbs in a large bowl.

In a separate bowl add mayonnaise and toss cooked corn through to coat.

Next, toss mayonnaise-coated corn through herb and cheese mix.

Serve with fresh lime.

PICKLED CUCUMBERS

(& EVERYTHING ELSE FROM THE GARDEN)

I take a pretty simple recipe for a pickling liquid and then chuck in just about anything I can lay my hands on from Jennee's garden or a local farm, leave it for a day or so and then bam

... you've got pickles.

BASIC PICKLING LIQUID

1lt (32 fl oz) white vinegar

200 g (7 oz) caster sugar

2 tbsp salt

Combine all ingredients and stir until sugar and salt have dissolved.

PICKLED RADISH

As much radish as you'd like to pickle

Pickle liquid (recipe on left)

Cut radishes into 4–6 wedges.

Cover with pickle liquid and set aside in the refrigerator for a day or two before using.

Dill Pickled Cucumber

1 kg (2 ¼ lb) cucumber, sliced

1 brown onion, sliced

1 tsp turmeric for a bit of color

A handful of chopped dill

Pickle liquid (recipe above)

Combine cucumber and onion with turmeric, dill and enough pickle liquid to cover.

Set aside in the refrigerator for a day or two before using.

Pickle will last for at least 1 month in the fridge. Leftover pickle liquid will last for ever.

Pickled Vegetables

1 head broccoli, cut into florets

½ head cauliflower, cut into florets

250 g (9 oz) green beans, trimmed and cut in half

2–3 baby onions, sliced

2 cloves garlic, sliced

½ long red chili, sliced

1 tsp yellow mustard seeds

Pickle liquid (recipe above left)

Combine all ingredients except pickle liquid.

Add pickle liquid to cover and set aside in the refrigerator for a day or two before using.

POTATO, ROASTED CARROT & CORN SALAD

(For the table)

500 g (17 ½ oz) Dutch cream potatoes, cut into large dice

300 g (10 ½ oz) small carrots

4 heads sweet corn, kernels removed from cob

3 spring onions (scallions), sliced

250 ml (8 fl oz) of mayonnaise (page 14)

1 tbsp apple cider vinegar

1 handful chopped parsley

Salt and pepper

Preheat oven to 200°C (400°F).

Boil or steam the potatoes.

Roast the carrots in oven until tender. Allow to cool and then slice into 1 cm (½ inch) pieces.

Flash the corn kernels in a hot pan with a little oil. 1 minute should do the trick. We just want to take them a level down from totally raw.

Get everything together in a large bowl and mix. Be a little gentle, so you don't crush the potatoes too much.

Season. Eat it.

I met Jennee 16 years ago. She was from the 'Coates' family and I am from the 'Stockdale' family. Like the Capulets and Montagues, it was clear that there would be staunch family pride involved in everything we did.

We started the great Coates/ Stockdale cook off early in the relationship and whenever our two families came together to laugh, fight, drink and eat we would drunkenly declare that the only way to find out who is better is through a cooking competition. The competition was fierce and extravagant and we have actually had to stop it due to the incredible time and pressure that we put on each other – the preparation for the comp has been known to go for days and comprise of 7 courses.

We now sit around lamenting the days that we beat each other and argue over memories that are embellished and, let's be honest, fairly hazy.

JENNEE'S CORN BREAD JAR SALAD

This particular recipe was created by the Coates team of Jennee and her sister Liz. It's an homage to the 1980s layered salad made famous by our mums (both Coates and Stockdale) during our childhoods.

It is also a sterling way to use up extra corn bread (page 40).

The key to this salad is to make many hours before so all the layers become set together like a terrine. With the cap of mayonnaise on top, it's sure to impress party goers at your next society ladies luncheon and will fit delightfully on the table sandwiched between the curried egg and lettuce sandwiches and devils on horseback.

You're going to need 4x 350 ml (12 fl oz) jars, or a large, clear salad bowl, so you may look in awe at the layers of deliciousness you have created.

(Serves 4 as a side)

4 slices corn bread, cut into 2cm (1 inch) dice

4 fire roasted red capsicum (bell pepper), chopped

2 cobs sweet corn, kernels removed from the cob, blanched for 2 minutes and then refreshed in cold water

2 dill pickles, diced

½ red onion, diced

½ iceberg lettuce, finely shredded

150 ml (5 fl oz) mayonnaise (page 14)

Paprika, to garnish

Chopped parsley, to garnish

Flash the corn kernels in a hot pan with a little oil. 1 minute should do the trick. We just want to take them a level down from totally raw.

In individual jars or salad bowl it's time to layer your salad.

Start with corn bread followed by corn,

Great lunch snack.

capsicum, pickles, onion, lettuce, and finally mayonnaise.

Garnish with a sprinkle of chopped parsley and a flick of paprika.

This salad is a nice little meal all by its lonesome, but also goes really well sitting next to a nice fat slice of smoked brisket (page 90) or with the roast chicken and chorizo (page 118).

MAKE A MAN A BURGER!

CHAPTER 3

A little thing I like to call

Burger-geddon

Make a man a burger and he shalt be happy for a day. Show a man how to make his own and he will be off your back forever.

I would just like to mention that it would not surprise me in the slightest if I married a burger one day (if I ever break up with Jennee, that is). I am in love with burgers and their seductive ways.

Maybe it would be wiser to open a burger joint … Recent studies have shown that half the people in the world love a good burger. Also, 50% of the people in the world make up half of the world's population. Also, I may not be basing these findings on any factual evidence of any kind. That's rock 'n' roll baby. On with the show.

Just one more little note; I like to use a slightly sweet and milky burger bun, but you can use whatever you want. I also like my bun opened up and just the inside toasted on the flat grill until the Maillard reaction has taken place and the outside is squishy enough to start to beckon you in.

CHEESE BURGER

(Serves 4)

4 burger buns

600 g (21 oz) beef mince

Salt and pepper

8 slices Monterey Jack or cheddar cheese

16–20 slices dill pickled cucumber (page 56)

4 slices raw onion

Ketchup (page 66)

American-style mustard

Form the mince into 4 fairly even burger patties. Press patties out to just over 1 cm thick. You can do this with the palm of your hand or a small frying pan or even grandma's old stove top iron.

Season patties with salt and pepper.

Fry or grill burgers for 2 minutes over high heat, flip and put 2 cheese slices on top of each patty. Cook for another two minutes for a medium result. Cook a little longer if you need it more well done.

Assemble burgers.

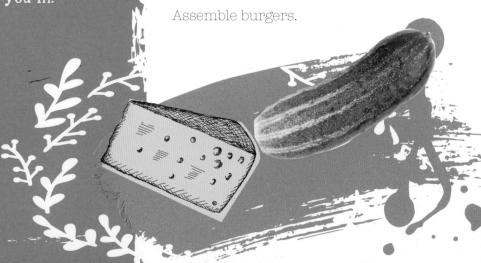

PULLED PORK BURGER

WITH 'SLAW, SPICY BALLS BBQ SAUCE & BBQ MUSTARD SAUCE

(Serves 4)

4 burger buns

600 g (21 oz) pulled pork (page 95)

Honky Dory 'slaw (page 32) or Kale and Apple 'slaw (page 35), both good here

Spicy Balls BBQ Sauce (page 18)

Barbecue Mustard Sauce (page 16)

Heat pork.

Put it all together.

TROPPO FRIED CHICKEN BURGER

(Serves 4)

4 burger buns

2 x 250 g (9 oz) chicken breasts, each sliced along the length into 2 thinner fillets

2 eggs, beaten

150 g (5 ½ oz) potato flour

2 tbls Big Red Rub (page 18)

Oil to deep fry

Big Red Seasoning (page 29)

4 slices smoked bacon, grilled

4 slices cheddar cheese

4 slices pineapple, fresh if you can, core removed and then grilled until slightly caramelized (that's the Troppo part)

Shredded iceberg lettuce

Mayonnaise (page 14)

Marinate the chicken in the Big Red Rub for an hour or two.

Roll the chicken through the egg mix and then the potato flour.

Give the chicken a little tap to remove excess flour.

Heat your oil in your deep fryer to 160°C (325°F).

Now fry the chicken for 4—5 minutes, until cooked.

Season the chicken with Big Red seasoning.

Need instructions about how to layer this bad boy? Let's start with mayonnaise on the top followed by lettuce. Now from the bottom we go bun, chicken, cheese, bacon and then pineapple.

SMOKED BRISKET CHEESE BURGER

WITH BARBECUE SAUCE, PICKLES & JALAPENOS AKA. THE TEXAS CHEESE BURGER

(Serves 4)

4 burger buns

600 g (21 oz) smoked brisket (page 90), sliced

4 slices Monterey Jack cheese

2 pickled jalapeño chilis, sliced

16 pieces dill pickled cucumber (page 56)

2–3 slices brown onion, chopped

BBQ sauce (page 17)

Divide ingredients between the buns, ensuring the cheese sits directly on the brisket to melt a little.
Serve.

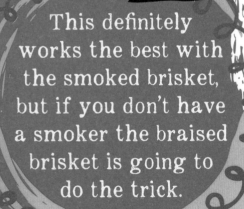

This definitely works the best with the smoked brisket, but if you don't have a smoker the braised brisket is going to do the trick.

Smoked brisket cheese burger

FISH BURGER

BEER BATTERED FISH BURGER

WITH KIMCHI

I recommend you talk to your local fishmonger about available fresh-caught fish that is good for frying.

(Serves 4)

4 burger buns

4x 125 g (4 ½ oz) fillets of fish

Beer batter (page 44)

125 g (4 ½ oz) plain flour

Shredded iceberg lettuce

250 ml (8 fl oz) kimchi (page 21)

16 pieces dill pickled cucumber (page 56)

Mayonnaise (page 14)

Salt and pepper

Get your frying oil up to 180°C (350°F).

Dredge the filets of fish through the flour and then into the batter.

Coat the fish in batter and scape across the side of the bowl slightly to ensure batter is not super thick.

Lower carefully into oil to avoid devastating burns and facial scarring.

Fry for 3—4 minutes, turning fish half way through.

Remove from oil and drain on absorbent paper.

Coat both sides of your bun with mayonnaise and layer the salad up however you see fit.

Season the fish and add to the bun to complete burger.

SOUTHERN FRIED EGGPLANT BURGER

(Serves 4)

This burger situation will convert even the most steadfast carnivore; it's a true story.

4 burger buns

1 medium eggplant (aubergine), sliced 1 cm (½ inch) thick – you'll need enough for 2 pieces per burger

250 g (9 oz) potato flour (starch)

2 eggs, whisked with a splash of water

8 onion rings (page 44)

Big Red Seasoning (page 29)

4 slices Monterey Jack or other cheese

Honky Dory 'Slaw (page 32)

Hot Sauce (page 19)

Alabama White BBQ Sauce (page 44)

Roll the eggplant (aubergine) through the egg mix and then the potato flour. You can repeat this process for a super crusty crust, AKA double crumbing, giving the eggplant a little pat afterwards to remove any excess flour.

Heat your oil to 180°C (350°F) give or take a degree or two.

Now fry the eggplant (aubergine) in batches. Four or five pieces at a time is probably good, for 3–4 minutes per batch, turning at the half way point.

Season with Big Red Seasoning mix.

Layer the whole lot up (from the bottom) – bun, eggplant (aubergine), cheese, onion rings, hot sauce, 'slaw, ranch dressing, then the top half of the bun.

How good is that for a veggie burger??

Southern Fried Vegetarian!

MEXICAN HANG-OVER ROLLS

(Serves 4)

First, I would like to make it clear that you do not need to be Mexican or have a hangover to enjoy these rolls … But if you do want a hangover to eat this roll, it is really quite easy to obtain one.

4 big rolls, or a full length Turkish pide (Yep. Go the pide if you can get hold of one. That is going to be the bossest way to do this)

3 smoked chorizo sausages, sliced

2 medium potatoes, boiled or steamed whole, cooled and cut into medium dice

2 red capsicums (bell peppers), diced

1 brown onion, diced

4 eggs (or 8 eggs for 2 each)

Herby Chili Oil (page 82)

A large handful of coriander (cilantro), parsley or watercress (or a combination of all three)

Salsa Picante (page 82), to serve

Sour cream, to serve

Chopped coriander (cilantro), to serve

Put chorizo, potato, capsicum (bell pepper) and onion into a large frying pan or baking pan, splash with some oil and pan fry or roast until it's starting to get some color and red oil is coming out of the chorizo.

When the chorizo and potato mix is done, fry your eggs. I like to fry mine with a good knob of butter and a splash of oil (if you need to fry your eggs in batches, do so, and set them aside until the sandwich goes together).

Slice the bread in half so you can fill it and then layer the chorizo mix on the bottom, followed by the eggs and a bit of seasoning. You can also add a bit of cheese if you're keen.

Place the lid on top and then cut into portions to cook. You can pan fry the portions or smash them in a sandwich press or even cook it as 1 big sandwich on a BBQ hot plate and portion it at the table.

Brush the top of the sandwich with Herby Chili Oil (page 82) and pan fry or cook in a sandwich press until they are looking mighty fine AKA golden and toasty.

Open the sandwich, add salsa, sour cream and coriander (cilantro) or other herbs.

Eat it. Great washed down with a Mexican beer, or tequila if you're feeling hard-core.

OYSTER PO' BO'

(Serves 4)

4 crusty baguette-style rolls

24 oysters

125 g plain flour

3 eggs, beaten with a splash of water

200 g panko breadcrumbs

4 slices good quality smoked bacon or prosciutto

Mayonnaise (page 14)

Fennel coleslaw (you can go with Honky Dory Coleslaw from page 32, just add a little finely sliced fennel in there too)

Salt and pepper

Smoked chili powder or Hot Sauce (page 19), to serve

Crumb oysters by first dredging in flour, then through the beaten egg mix and then through the breadcrumbs.

Heat the oil in a pan over medium heat to shallow fry oysters.

Once oil is at 180°C (350°F), gently place oysters into pan and fry for 1 minute or so each side, until golden. Remove from pan and drain on kitchen paper.

Season oysters with salt and pepper.

Discard oil from the pan and then fry bacon until crisp.

Spread some mayonnaise in your bun, followed by fennel 'slaw, oysters, bacon and smoked chili powder or Hot Sauce.

Oyster po' bo's … or as my boys like to call them: oysters burgers. They can call them what they wish – as long as a receptacle of glutinous origins is going to be transporting some fried oysters to my face, possibly with some coleslaw to aid the journey… whenever these are on the menu, I'm only concerned with making sure I get my fair share before they're eaten by my oyster-loving children.

Enter the smoked chili powder. I made this quite simply by chucking some long red chilis into the smoker for about 30 minutes, followed by a few days on a drying rack and then grinding them into a powder. I shall be liberally dusting this smoked chili powder over my fried oysters as soon as they emerge from their exfoliating and rejuvenating 180°C (350°F) burning hot oil bath. Sometimes, as a parent, you need to pull a few little tricks out to ensure to get your share – or a share – or just some table scraps! Cunning, right? I'm just scared of the day my children pass Chili Appreciation 101 …

81

HERBY CHILI OIL

1 tsp dried chili flakes

1 tsp dried oregano

1 tsp dried thyme

2 tbsp olive oil

Put all ingredients into a bowl and mix. Simple is best.

SALSA PICANTE

4 ripe tomatoes, charred over a flame until they start to blacken and blister

1 eschalot (shallot/French shallot) or half an onion, finely diced

2 cloves garlic, crushed

2 pickled jalapeño chili, chopped

1 tbsp of the jalapeño vinegar

Salt and pepper

Peel the blackened skin from the tomatoes.

Put everything into a food processor and pulse into a chunky salsa texture.

Salsa will last sealed in the fridge for 1 week, but you will eat it with corn chips watching the home shopping channel well before then.

REUBEN-ISH SANDWICH OR BURGER

(Serves 4)

8 slices bread or 4 burger buns

16 slices pastrami

12 slices decent ham

4 slices Swiss cheese

400 g (14 oz) sauerkraut (page 22)

A good slather of Russian-esque dressing (recipe page 85)

Dill pickles, to serve

For toasted sandwich style: put everything together between two slices of quality bread (rye is traditional, but you can use whatever bread you like), get a little butter and oil in a pan over medium heat and then fry sandwich for 3 or so minutes each side until browned and toasty and warm.

For the burger style: heat the meats through in a pan over medium flame. Once warmed pile meats on top of each other so they will fit in your bun and put cheese on top to melt a little. Put meat pile onto base of burger bun, put sauerkraut on top and then Russian Dressing.

RUSSIAN-ESQUE DRESSING

250 ml (8 fl oz) Mayonnaise (page 14)

60 ml (2 fl oz) tomato ketchup

½ small onion, diced

3 dill pickles, diced (page 56)

2 tsp American-style mustard

1 tsp Worcestershire sauce

1 tsp Hot Sauce (page 19)

Pulse all ingredients in a food processor until combined, or chop the onion and pickles nice and fine and mix it all together in a bowl.

Leftover dressing is really good to dip hot chips into, or pretty much just put it on everything. It will last sealed in the fridge for 1 week.

REALLY PORKY TACOS

(Serves 4)

400 g (14 oz) pork belly, sliced into 3 cm thick pieces

2 morcilla, black pudding or other kind of blood sausage

2 smoked chorizo sausages

The first time I presented these tacos, I was caught a little off guard by my family's sudden embrace of the blood sausage component and their zealous consumption of a good percentage of it. Normally, I get to eat the blood sausage around here. These things are good. Really good.

I would also recommend giving the homemade tortillas a try. They're well worth the effort!

1 chipotle chili, if you like it hot, very finely chopped

Salt and pepper

Soft Tacos (page 86)

Salsa Picante (page 82)

Sliced radish, chopped onion, coriander (cilantro) and lime wedges, to serve

Cook the meats over low coals. Keep in mind that the pork belly is going to take a lot longer than the sausages, as they are already cooked.

Once cooked to your liking, chop it all up. Get two knives out and do it like a cartoon Asian chef if that makes you feel good about yourself. Chuck the chipotle in there too – chop it all in together.

Adjust seasoning if necessary.

That's it, get it on the table.

SOFT TACOS

(Makes 20 tacos, so maybe you have enough for some quesadillas for lunch tomorrow)

375 g (13 oz) masa harina* flour

400 ml (13 fl oz) hot water

In a medium bowl, mix together masa harina and hot water until thoroughly combined. Turn dough onto a clean surface and knead until pliable and smooth. If dough is dry add more hot water.

Cover dough tightly with cling wrap (plastic film) and allow to stand for 30 minutes. If it dries out while resting, sprinkle with more water.

Preheat a frying pan to medium-high.

Divide dough into 20 equal-size balls. Using a tortilla press, a rolling pin or your hands, press each ball of dough flat between two sheets of baking paper.

Place tortilla in preheated pan and allow to cook for approximately 30 seconds, or until browned and slightly puffy. Turn tortilla over to brown on second side for approximately 30 seconds more and then transfer to a plate. Repeat process with each ball of dough. Wrap tortillas with a towel to stay warm and moist until ready to serve.

*You'll probably need to go to a fancy or culturally relevant shop to buy masa harina, or specific corn flour used to make tortillas or tacos.

Lunch choices!

Smoking or grilling whichever way you like!

CHAPTER 4

The meaty, grilly, smoky side of things

Sometimes, as a gentleman, you just need to eat yourself a big hunk of meat and gnaw it straight from the bone …

... often, I even go that little bit further and cook it first, just to really treat myself. And, if I want to truly venture out into the realm that is 'the next level', that aforementioned meat is going to be kissed and licked by flames and touched by the golden hand of smoky, smoky goodness.

Smoking or even grilling meat on your BBQ, Weber, or something else that involves coals and a few wood chips or twigs, is something that you really need to feel. It is something that would take me more than a page of a book to explain to you. But rest assured, I will explain what I can and I will hold your hand as we stroll casually through the intricacies of the techniques and methods needed to master the grilling of pork ribs ... or steak ... or chicken ... or anything else for that matter.

The rest is up to you.

Get practicing!

SMOKED BRISKET

(For a gathering of the hungry man's club)

4 - 5 kg (9—11 lb) beef brisket

500 ml (16 fl oz) strong black coffee (for the oven version)

Salt and pepper

Crushed Hominy with Brisket Gravy (page 93), Honky Dory 'slaw (page 32) and BBQ Sauce (page 17) make nice sides to serve with the brisket. But so do pretty much all of the other sides on these pages, so take your pick.

For the smoker:

Season beef well with salt and pepper.

Get your smoker up to 125°C (250°F).

Get the brisket into your smoker, making sure you keep a fairly constant 125°C (250°F).

After 4—5 hours the brisket should have an internal temperature of 65—70°C (150°F) or so. This is when I like to wrap it.

Remove the brisket and wrap it with aluminum foil. Return to the smoker for another 3—4 hours or until the internal temperature at the thickest part of the brisket is 92—95°C (200°F). You will need a probe thermometer for this. This is definitely as specific as I get with cooking and there is a reason for that ... this is how you make it really good!

Once the brisket is at 92—95°C (200°F) remove from smoker and rest for 1 hour.

Now, and only now, it is time to eat your brisket.

SMOKY GOODNESS

Get some sides together, get some sauce and serve.

For the oven (this is not BBQ):

Marinate the beef in coffee overnight or at least a few hours.

Season well with salt and pepper and roast, covered, in a 150°C (300°F) oven for 5 or so hours or until very tender. If the liquid dries up before meat is cooked, add a little water, 1 cup at a time until soft and melting. This is also a grand opportunity to pull out your slow cooker and let the beef simmer away for the day in that.

Once that piece of beefy goodness is done, set it aside and allow to cool for a bit.

Now slice it up (or shred it for pulled beef) the best you can and serve it with some sides that are going to make you happy.

Save those pan juices for the Brisket Gravy (page 93).

CRUSHED HOMINY WITH BRISKET GRAVY

(For the table)

This is one of those sides that is simple and delicious. Simply delicious. You can use store-bought beef stock for your gravy and store-bought chicken stock for the crushed hominy if you really want, otherwise keep it fully legit and use the leftover pan juices for the brisket gravy and some homemade chicken stock for the hominy.

3x 400g (14 oz) tins hominy (dried maize (corn) kernels treated with an alkaline solution), strained

1 brown onion, diced

2 cloves garlic, crushed

600 ml (1 pint) chicken stock (store-bought or use the recipe for Chicken Gravy at page 30)

Salt and pepper

Heat a pot large enough to hold everything over medium flame.

Sauté onion and garlic with a little oil until soft.

Add hominy and stock, and season with salt and pepper.

Simmer for 15—20 minutes.

Blitz with stick whizz or mash. Texture should be slightly chunky, not completely smooth.

Check seasoning and adjust if necessary.

Serve with gravy. Brisket gravy if possible (recipe below) but Chicken Gravy (page 30) will certainly do the trick.

BRISKET GRAVY

1 L (32 fl oz) brisket braising juice (from braised brisket recipe page 90) or good quality beef stock

50 g (2 oz) plain flour

Salt and pepper

Heat braising juices or beef stock to a simmer.

Make a slurry out of the flour and ½ a cup of water.

Whisking constantly, slowly add ¾ of the flour slurry to the stock, reserving a little to adjust thickness if necessary.

Continue to simmer and stir gravy for 2–3 minutes to cook out the flour.

Check the viscosity. If it is a little thick you can whisk in a splash of water to thin it out. If it is a little thin you can whisk in the remaining slurry and cook it out for another couple of minutes.

Check seasoning and adjust with salt and pepper if necessary.

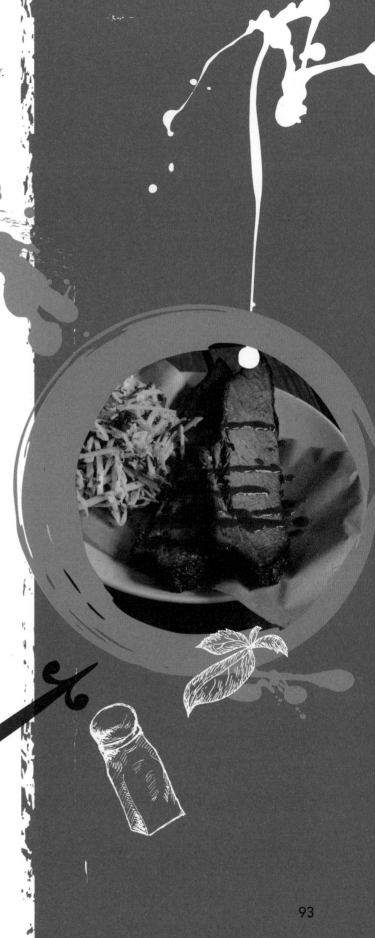

LEGIT AS HECK PULLED PORK

WITH BIG RED RUB

(Serves 6—8)

This stuff is the goods. Whether it be with jerk spice, a tasty Asian inspired marinade or the traditional American Smokehouse style, you should embrace the pulling of the pork.

Do it. Eat it now.

2–3 kg (4 ½–6 ½ lb) pork neck or shoulder (remove skin if using shoulder, but save it for crackling)

225 g (8 oz) Big Red Rub (page 18)

Salt and pepper

250 ml (8 fl oz) apple juice

Carolina mustard sauce (page 16), to serve

For the smoker:

Coat the pork with the Big Red Rub. Give it a nice little massage to really cover it.

Get your smoker up to 125°C (250°F).

Get the pork into your smoker, making sure you keep a fairly constant 125°C (250°F). Give your pork a nice little spray with the apple juice every hour.

After 3–4 hours it's time to wrap the pork.

Remove the pork from the smoker, give it one last spritz with apple juice and wrap it with aluminum foil. Return to the smoker for another 1–2 hours or until the internal temperature is 92–95°C (200°F). You will need a probe thermometer for this.

Once temperature is at 92–95°C (200°F), remove from smoker and rest for 1 hour.

Now place whole package in a tray or pan to catch liquid gold juices.

Unwrap and pull pork into nicely shredded strands.

Pour juices back over pork, adjust seasoning with salt and pepper if necessary and get that pork on the table

… But not before you've stood there for a few seconds to truly absorb what you have just done.

Carolina mustard sauce is a good place to start when serving this stuff.

For the oven (this is not BBQ):

Coat the pork with the Big Red Rub. Give it a nice little massage.

Place it in a baking dish and cover it with a lid, or a piece of wood or aluminium foil.

Get that dish into a medium oven; 160°C (325°F) should do the trick, for somewhere around the 3–4 hour mark (you could also use a slow cooker). Check it after three hours and if that thing isn't quivering like jelly, then simply whack it back into the oven for another half an hour … and another after that until fully cooked. Once it is ready, you will be able to prod it a little and watch as it yields beneath your finger.

Pull it out and onto a cutting board. Put your knife across the grain 3 or 4 times and then run your fingers through it to finish the shredding.

Return the pork to the cooking liquid, check seasoning and serve with some sides of your choosing, starting with Carolina mustard sauce.

PULLED PORK HASH

(serves 4)

This recipe was born from a stash of last night's leftovers and an appetite for destruction, and it's a breakfast that lures me in every time.

600 g (21 oz) leftover pulled pork, corned beef or bacon.

3–4 cooked potatoes, diced

1 brown onion, diced

16 cherry tomatoes, halved

A large handful parsley, torn

Salt and pepper

Eggs cooked how you like them, to serve

BBQ sauce (page 17), to serve

Hot Sauce (page 19), to serve

Toast, to serve

Heat a splash of oil in a pan, add potatoes and fry on medium heat until they start to brown.

Add onions and fry for another minute.

Add a knob of butter and pork, and fry for one more minute.

Remove from the heat, add tomatoes

and parsley and toss to combine.

Season with salt and pepper.

Hopefully now your eggs and toast are ready and you can serve it all up together, there's nothing worse than being made to wait for breakfast, especially as morning small talk is not usually the sharpest.

PULLED PORK

WITH CHINESE FLAVORS

(Serves 6—8)

While we're on the pulled pork, here's another flavor. Same method as the recipe page 95 just with a different marinade.

2–3 kg (4 ½–6 ½ lb) piece of pork neck or shoulder (skin removed)

60 ml (2 fl oz) light soy sauce

60 ml (2 fl oz) oyster sauce

60 ml (2 fl oz) Shaoxing cooking wine*

60 ml (2 fl oz) Chinese black vinegar

1 brown onion, diced

10 cloves garlic, crushed

1 thumb-sized knob ginger, sliced

2 star anise

1 cinnamon stick

4 cardamom pods, crushed slightly

with the flat of a knife

3 cloves, crushed slightly with the flat of a knife

1 tsp ground white pepper

250 ml (8 fl oz) chicken stock or water

Mix everything, except the pork and stock/water, to make a marinade.

Rub all over the pork and put it in the fridge to do its thing. Overnight is ideal, but at least 3–4 hours is good. If you don't marinate it, it will still work out A-OK.

Whack the pork and all the marinade juices in an oven dish and cover. Add the stock/water and cook at 150°C (300°F) for 3–4 hours, or until the meat will push apart very easily. A slow cooker

would also do the job here (get it on first thing in the morning for dinner that evening).

Pull the meat out of the juices and into a bowl for the shredding action. All going according to plan, the meat will be so tender it will yield under the pressure of the tongs or your hands and you will end up with many smaller chunks.

Let it cool a little, but while it is still warm shred the meat up with two forks, or a fork and some tongs, or your fingers.

Strain the juices and pour over pork.

Eat this one with rice, or in a sandwich, or however you want to really – it is your pork after all.

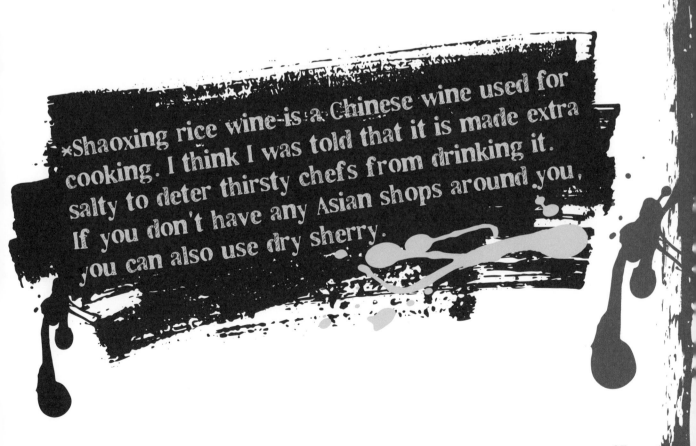

*Shaoxing rice wine is a Chinese wine used for cooking. I think I was told that it is made extra salty to deter thirsty chefs from drinking it. If you don't have any Asian shops around you, you can also use dry sherry.

PORK RIBS

(PURPOSE BUILT SMOKER)

(Serves 4)

After three hours in the depths of the smoky abyss, these ribs come out tanned, tender and delicious, and you would be more than happy to show them to your friends and let them have a little chew too. These ribs leave a damn fine taste in your mouth and have you wanting more.

The taste of smoky goodness mixed with the elation of chewing a damn fine piece of meat from the bone, some of my favorite sides and a kick-ass BBQ glaze make me a happy, happy man.

2x 1 ¼–1 ½ kg (2 ¾–3 ½ lb) racks pork spare ribs or St Louis trimmed ribs

150 g (5 oz) Big Red Rub (page 18) or your favorite rib rub

250 ml (8 fl oz) apple juice

50 g (2 oz) butter

2 tbsp brown sugar

BBQ Sauce (page 17)

Sexy Corn (page 55), to serve

BBQ Pit Beans (page 102), to serve

Get your smoker up to 125°C (250°F).

Season ribs generously with Big Red Rub (or your favorite rib rub).

Smoke the ribs for 2 hours at 125°C (250°F). Spritz twice with apple juice.

Remove ribs from smoker and place meaty side up, each on a separate sheet of aluminum foil. Rub ribs with butter and then sprinkle with sugar. Wrap tightly with foil.

Return ribs to smoker for another hour, ensuring that the temperature is still hovering around the 125°C (250°F) mark.

After an hour remove ribs from smoker and set aside for 5 minutes so they are not searing hot.

Unwrap ribs and return to smoker, meaty side up. Glaze ribs with BBQ sauce and cook for another 15 minutes to set the glaze, glazing once more after 8–10 minutes. Alternatively, if you'd like a drier rib, do not glaze them and just return them to the smoker for 15 minutes to dry out the bark a little.

Once ready, slice and serve with Sexy Corn and BBQ Pit Beans.

BIG RED

Rub

Smoky Goodness

GHETTO SMOKED PORK RIBS

So it may or may not come as a surprise to you, but I do not carry a barbeque wherever I travel, but oft the occasion does arise where I find myself donning someone else's kitchen apron and getting saucy with whatever barbeque apparatus it is that they may have.

How though? What if you want a bit of smoky goodness and the only tool available is a gas, or even worse, an electric version of what should be a BBQ? What are you gonna do? Ghetto Smokehouse to the rescue! What is Ghetto Smokehouse, you ask?

Read on my friends, read on...

The Ghetto Smoker

To get your 'Ghetto Smoker' up and running you need a barbeque with a lid, woodchips or a few chunks of fruit wood (hickory is good and also available at just about every barbeque store or the larger hardware stores, but there are heaps of other woods you can use) and a little aluminum foil.

Wrap a few large handfuls of wood chips (fruit wood chunks will not need to be wrapped) in a little foil basket/package. That little package goes next to a low-medium flame on the grill bars until it starts smoking, and then your ribs, or whatever it is that you want to be smoking, go on the hot plate or grill bars just next to it. Once again, you want to have little to no heat at all directly under your ribs; they are going to get most of their heat from the BBQ flame once the lid goes down. If you put the heat up, things can go pear shaped pretty damn quickly, so keep the heat low.

Pork Ribs (Ghetto Smoker)

It's all exactly the same as a purpose built smoker (page 98), just using the ghetto beast!

NB: You want the temperature inside the chamber to be 125°C (250°F). If it's getting a little cool, turn the indirect heat up a little (not the heat under the ribs). When the wood chips burn out, put some fresh wood chips back in to ensure your smoky satisfaction. It may seem too hard, but seriously it's worth the extra effort.

BBQ PIT BEANS

(This is enough for a barbeque plus some for the freezer to save for breakfast)

Pit beans (or smoky baked beans as you might call them) are a fully feasible side for a barbecue. It's true. And if you don't believe me, eat them for breakfast with some sausages and eggs.

1 kg (2 ¼ lb) dried navy or pinto beans, soaked overnight and then simmered until tender

250 ml (8 fl oz) tomato paste

150 ml (5 fl oz) tomato ketchup

100 g (3 ½ oz) brown sugar

60 ml (2 fl oz) maple syrup

2 tbsp American-style mustard

2 tbsp apple cider vinegar

3 tbsp Big Red Rub (page 18) or your favorite BBQ rub

1 tbsp onion powder

1 tbsp garlic powder

1 tbsp dried thyme

1 tbsp hot sauce

1 tbsp salt

½ tbsp pepper

2 l (4 ¼ pints) water

Combine everything except beans in a mixing bowl and stir until mixed thoroughly. Add beans, stir to combine and pour into a large baking pan or casserole dish.

This goes into your smoker at 125°C (250°F) for 3 hours for the preferred, smoky version, or into the oven at 160°C (325°F) for an hour or so will get the job done.

Pit beans are great served with any BBQ. Remaining beans should be frozen down in easily defrostable packs for later use.

LAMB RIBS

(Serves 4)

A damn good ribbing …

No, we're not going to be poking fun at each other. We shall be cooking up a favorite of my family; lamb ribs.

It is important to remember that lamb ribs are definitely not pork ribs, but they are still damn tasty in the smoker and something a little different for your next BBQ. They can also offer that same sort of smoky, ribby wow factor but at a cheaper price tag than pork or beef ribs – that is, until the butchers work out that they are just as tasty as their high-end friends and bump the price up on these puppies too. But for the time being, these things have a great cost to flavor ratio.

The only way to eat these is with chimichurri sauce and with pearl barley, carrot and feta salad.

DAMN GOOD RIBBING

2x 1 ¼ kg (2 ¾ lb) racks lamb ribs

1 tbsp dried oregano

1 tbsp dried thyme

1 tbsp ground cumin seed

1 tbsp sumac

1 tbsp garlic granules

2 tbsp brown sugar

2 tbsp salt

1 tsp dried chili flakes

½ tsp ground black pepper

250 ml apple juice, in spray bottle

Chimichurri sauce (page 19), to serve

Pearl barley, carrot and feta salad (next recipe), to serve

In a bowl, combine everything except lamb and apple juice, and mix to combine for your lamb rub.

Rub lamb down with a splash of vegetable oil, to help your rub adhere, and then coat with rub. Remaining rub can be stored in an air tight container for a few weeks and used on chicken or roasted vegetables.

Give the lamb ribs 3 hours in a smoker at 125°C (250°F) with the occasional spritz with the apple juice spray.

I find that lamb ribs don't need to be wrapped because they are pretty fatty. It's nice for them to crust up a little more and for the fat to render out and make a delicious little parcel of lamb goodness for you to devour.

Serve with chimichurri sauce and pearl barley, carrot and feta salad.

It is very worthy of note that any leftover smoked lamb ribs are magical when crumbed (breaded) and then fried for 3—4 minutes. Actually, it is truly worth cooking an extra rack or two just so you may try this.

PEARL BARLEY, ROASTED CARROT & FETA SALAD

(Serves 4)

Yes. I really do enjoy the sweet, sweet taste of roasted carrots.

200 g (7 oz) pearl barley, simmered until tender

6 medium carrots

6 eschalots (French shallots) or baby onions

100 g (3 ½ oz) feta cheese, crumbled

2 spring onions or shallots (scallions), finely sliced

1 handful parsley, coarsely chopped

1 handful mint, coarsely chopped

Salt and pepper

Apple cider vinaigrette (page 17), to dress

Oil and season the carrots and whole eschalots (French shallots) or baby onions. Roast in a 200°C (400°F) oven for 15—20 minutes or until tender. Allow to cool.

Slice carrot into 1 cm (½ inch) pieces, and onions into quarters.

Combine salad ingredients, season and dress with a splash of apple cider vinaigrette.

BACON WRAPPED JALAPEÑO POPPERS

STUFFED WITH TALEGGIO

(For the table or for just you to enjoy with a beer)

150 g (5 oz) cream cheese

50 g (2 oz) taleggio cheese or other washed rind cheese

12 fresh jalapeño chilis, sliced in half lengthways and a few seeds scraped out, kept in pairs

24 slices of belly bacon, speck or pancetta

Toothpicks or skewers

Mix cheeses in a food processor until combined.

Scoop a spoonful of mixture into each half of jalapeño. and then gently push back together.

Wrap chili with bacon and skewer though the middle to secure chili and prevent cheese from flowing out all over the place , ensuring the join is on the underside of the chili so it doesn't unravel during cooking.

Smoke jalapeños in a preheated 125°C (250°F) smoker or grill for 1 hour or until jalapeño softens a little.

NANA ROSE'S POTATO SALAD

(For the table)

My Nana's salad uses potato, Polski Ogorki (Polish dill pickles), smoked Polish sausage, brown onion, boiled egg, white pepper and vinegar. When I'm in need of a nostalgia fix, I will follow her recipe to the letter. Other times I will wing it a little and add a bit of Mayonnaise, different meat, nuts or herbs. If my Grandad were still here, he would look at me and say 'What are you doing boy?' in his still excellent Polish accent, then he would chuckle to himself and go back to within a foot of the TV to watch the next half of the West Coast Eagles' game. My Grandad loved the West Coast Eagles, and he didn't see very well.

1 kg Desiree potatoes, boiled in their skin, whole, until tender (the potato should slide off easily when you insert a knife), then use a paring knife to peel them while they're still hot, and then cut into bite sized cubes

1 brown onion, peeled and diced

4—5 dill pickles, diced

200 g (7 oz) smoked Polish sausage (substitute speck), diced

5 boiled eggs, peeled and chopped

Salt and a good hit of white pepper

A good splash of white wine vinegar or the liquid from the pickles

½ bunch of parsley, chopped

The main requirement for making this is to mix everything while the potatoes are still warm so all of the ingredients can have a little party and their flavors can really get to know each other.

Nana Rose!

MA'S TOMATO, ONION SALAD

(For the table)

This would make an appearance at every Sunday BBQ we ever had. Along with its brethren, the potato salad and coleslaw, and its lesser recognised cousins, the watermelon salad and curried rice salad. It is simple and tasty and has the potential to make the bearer look good. The secret is to dress and season it a bit before serving so all the juices of the salad ingredients get drawn out to help form the dressing. I put a bit of olive oil in mine just to zhuzh it up a bit but I'm not sure if Ma would condone my actions. I'm sure she wouldn't mind a bit of parsley in there though …

3—4 ripe tomatoes, sliced

1 large cucumber, sliced

1 brown onion, sliced

3 tbsp white wine vinegar

Salt and pepper

A splash of olive oil

1 tbsp chopped parsley, to garnish

You pretty much just put this whole thing together in a mixing bowl 15 minutes before you want to serve it so it can macerate and free all of its lovely juices.

MA'S RISSOLES

(Serves 4)

Mum's rissoles are a fond childhood memory; when eating them or even thinking about them, they remind me of my midnight missions to the fridge on rissole night when I was vegetarian. There was no way in the world that I was going to be able to stand true to my animal loving convictions with these things in the house. Believe me I still love animals, I just prefer some of them to come with a side of tomato sauce (ketchup).

Mum is not the most adventurous of cooks. It's only recently that I have started forcing her to eat 'weird' or 'different' food and push the limits further than meat 'n' three veg or 'spag bol', but Mum's rissoles were a favorite. Whether hot, warm or cold with tomato sauce on sangers** the next day, they were always great.

1 kg (2¼ lb) beef mince

250 ml (8 fl oz) cooked rice

1 brown onion, finely diced

1 carrot, grated

1 egg, whisked

A handful of chopped parsley

Salt and pepper

200 g (7 oz) panko breadcrumbs

Tomato ketchup (page 15), to serve

Cooked vegetables, to serve

Mix it all together and season with a good hit of salt and pepper.

Form into 4–6 patties, depending on how big you like them.

Roll through breadcrumbs and pat into surface of rissoles.

Cook in an oiled pan over low-medium heat for 5 minutes on each side or until cooked through.

Serve with three veg, boiled for a bit too long, and tomato ketchup, or cold in white bread sandwiches, also with tomato ketchup.

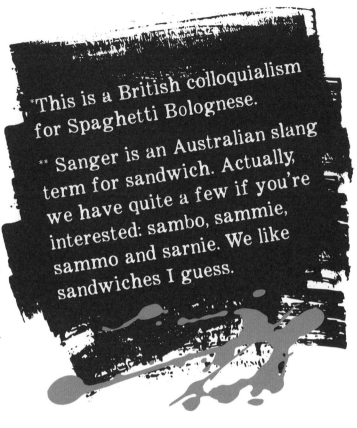

*This is a British colloquialism for Spaghetti Bolognese.

** Sanger is an Australian slang term for sandwich. Actually, we have quite a few if you're interested: sambo, sammie, sammo and sarnie. We like sandwiches I guess.

TEX-MEX SPICE MIX

2 tbsp ground cumin

2 tbsp dried thyme

2 tbsp dried oregano

1 tbsp dried chili flakes

Mix it all together and store extra in an airtight container for your next Tex Mex feast.

Chili is pretty simple. I am pretty simple. This is going to work out just fine.

The thing about beef shin is that it scares a lot of people; it doesn't conjure up images of fun times and you know the results are something that could be terrible at best. The one thing you need to know about beef shin is it turns out so damn good if you give it a bit of low and slow love. Cooking a beef shin like this is a pretty sure-fire way to end up with a cracking beefy meal. The gelatinousness of the beef shin can only be described as luxurious, with a possible secondary reference to it being unctuous ... and those of you who know me know for a fact that those are words that I'm only going to use when all other avenues have been exhausted. Beef shin, when cooked properly, is a damn fine experience for all. Or possibly just the person eating it.

So this is what I am giving to the human race to make the world a happier, safer and just gosh-darn nicer place to be. Unless you are vegetarian. If you are vegetarian, you will probably not enjoy this so much. This is my oh-so-beefy, gelatinous, unctuous and cheesy chili.

BEEF SHIN & BEER CHILI CON CARNE

(This ingredient list is enough for a few cowboys - easily 8-10 people)

1 big beef shin, 1.5 kg (3½ lb).

Get your butcher to cut it in half or in thirds (you can also use leftover smoked beef brisket for this recipe – you will only need to simmer it for a couple of hours if you do this)

2 brown onions, diced

1 red or green capsicum (bell pepper), diced

5 cloves garlic, chopped

4 tbsp Tex-Mex spice mix (recipe follows)

2 chipotle chili in adobo, plus a splash of the sauce they come in

1 cinnamon stick

750 ml beer (whatever you drink will work fine)

3x 400 g (14 oz) tins crushed tomatoes or tomato passata

2x 400 g (14 oz) tin black beans (or kidney beans)

3 pieces good dark chocolate

Salt and pepper

Fried tortillas, to serve

Avocado and tomato salsa, to serve

Shredded cheese, to serve

Sour cream, to serve

Get a nice big pot out for this one.

Season beef shin and sauté in a little oil until it starts to get some color.

Add onions, capsicum, garlic, Tex-Mex spice, chipotle and cinnamon. Cook out for a few minutes until onion and capsicum are soft.

Add beer, tomatoes and beans, and simmer on really low heat for 3 hours, stirring regularly. This could also be a slow cooker moment if that's how you roll.

Check if beef is tender by pushing a bit from the bone. If it's not, simmer for another half an hour until meat is falling from the bone.

Once the beef is tender, remove from the pot, allow to cool a little and then shred.

Get the chocolate into the pot.

Return beef to the pot, check seasoning and serve however you like. We went for fried tortilla chips, a simple avocado and tomato salsa, shredded cheese and some sour cream.

tomato

REALLY SIMPLE SMOKED SALMON

(Serves 4)

800 g (28 oz) piece of Atlantic Salmon or Ocean Trout

Salt and pepper

Olive oil

Lemon

Ranch dressing (page 15), to serve

Braised green beans, to serve

Potato salad (page 106), to serve

No secrets here. You light up your smoker and get it to 110°C (230°F).

Season the fish with salt and pepper.

Place it in the smoker, skin side down, and cook for 30—40 minutes, until desired done-ness is achieved. Still soft to touch and moist in the middle is a good medium rare. The firmer the fillet, the more cooked the fish will be.

Splash the fish with a little olive oil and the juice of a lemon, and let it sit for 5 minutes. As tempting as it is to eat right away, this will really improve the meal and is worth the wait.

Now it's time to break it four pieces and serve.

Remaining salmon is great tossed through pasta or with avocado and fresh curd on toast for breakfast.

PRAWNS WITH MANGO 'SLAW

(Serves 4)

I've based this very loosely on the classic prawn cocktail, but made a bit of a mango 'slaw instead of the old iceberg lettuce scenario. Even if you're not really a fan of mango in a savoury meal, I recommend you give it a go; once you try it you pretty quickly realise how wrong you were. It's really good, especially graced with the presence of a pile of big, fat, fresh king prawns.

20 good quality cooked prawns (or grab some fresh prawns and grill them over the coals)

⅛ green cabbage, shredded or sliced with a mandoline if you have one

1 carrot, grated

2 mango, sliced

1 tbsp pickled ginger, chopped

2 spring onion (shallot/scallion), sliced, plus extra to garnish

A splash of lemon juice

Salt and pepper

Cocktail sauce (page 116), to serve

Combine everything except prawns and cocktail sauce.

Put the salad in a bowl.

Hit it with a couple of tablespoons of cocktail sauce.

Give the prawns a nice home on top of the salad.

Garnish it with a few extra sliced spring onions (shallot/scallion)

SEAFOOD & CORN CHOWDER

(Serves 6)

I know this is one of the most obvious things a person could say when putting a recipe for any type of rustic soup in a cook book but do make sure you have heaps of crusty bread on hand to mop up when you're done. You can use any leftover smoked salmon from page 113 in this recipe, or make extra to use in chowder.

400 g (14 oz) firm fresh fish of your choice, 2 cm (1 inch) dice

200 g (7 oz) smoked salmon, flaked into large chunks

300 g (10 ½ oz) fresh prawn meat

6 rashers bacon, chopped

1 brown onion, cut into 1 cm dice

1 carrot, cut into 1 cm dice

1 stick celery, sliced

4 cobs fresh sweet corn, kernels removed

1 large potato, cut into 1 cm dice

2 cloves garlic, minced

1 tsp dried thyme

A pinch of smoked chili powder or cayenne, plus extra to garnish

1 L(2 pints) thickened cream

250 ml (8 fl oz) full cream milk

Salt and pepper

Chopped parsley, to garnish

Crusty bread, to serve

In a large pot sauté the bacon, onions, carrot, celery, potato, garlic, thyme and chili powder.

Once it is softened and starting to color add the milk and cream and simmer until potatoes are just cooked. This should take about 20 minutes.

Add the fresh fish, prawns and corn and simmer for another 5 minutes. Stir it a couple of times but do it gently so you don't break the fish up.

Remove from heat and stir through smoked salmon.

Check and adjust seasoning.

Serve garnished with parsley and extra smoked chili powder, and crusty bread on the side.

SMOKED FISH & POTATO SALAD

(Serves 4 as a light lunch)

You can pretty easily smoke your own fish (page 113) for this recipe too.

400 g (14 oz) smoked fish, broken into chunks

4 medium Dutch cream potatoes, diced and cooked until tender

A few handfuls of croutons (about 4 bread slices' worth)

1 carrot, finely diced

6 radish, sliced

1 handful rocket (arugula)

Salt and pepper

Dill Ranch Dressing (page 15)

In a large bowl, mix everything except the dressing together.

Add enough dressing to lightly coat.

Check seasoning.

Divide into 4 bowls and serve.

COCKTAIL SAUCE

250 ml (8 fl oz) mayonnaise (page 14)

60 ml (2 fl oz) tomato Ketchup (page 15)

A splash of Tabasco or Hot Sauce (page 19)

A splash of Worcestershire sauce

A splash of brandy

Salt and pepper

Combine all ingredients in a mixing bowl.

Mix it all up – a whisk is a great tool to help you with this job.

Any remaining sauce will last in the refrigerator for up to 1 week.

MOJO CHICKEN

WITH PIÑA COLADA SALSA

Yes, we're back to the salsa thing. Summer is all about the salsa for me, I am so into it that I am actually considering enrolling for salsa dancing lessons just so there is more salsa in my life … A good salsa will spice up your dinner table and is always welcome with my Mojo chicken.

I have also done a mojo ham for Christmas lunch, which was a bit different but delicious.

Mojo Chicken

(Serves 6)

6 chicken marylands. Roughly 1½ kg (3½ lb)

125 ml (4 fl oz) fresh orange juice, plus the zest of 1 orange

60 ml (2 fl oz) fresh lime juice, plus the zest of 1 lime

4 cloves garlic, crushed

2 tsp dried oregano

1 tsp ground cumin

1 tsp dried chili flakes

A splash of olive oil

Salt and pepper

Piña colada salsa (recipe following), to serve

Mix everything together in a large bowl and leave to marinate for 30 minutes.

This is really good cooked over medium-low coals for 40 minutes or so, turning regularly and basting with the remaining marinade.

If you have neither the fire nor technology needed to cook the chicken on the coals, a hot oven will do the trick. 200°C (400°F) for 40 minutes, basting and turning regularly.

Piña Colada Salsa

½ medium fresh pineapple, diced (you need 2 cups or so of diced pineapple)

2 spring onions (shallots/scallions), sliced

3 tbsp shredded coconut

60 ml (2 fl oz) coconut cream

½ long green chili, deseeded and diced finely

10 - 12 mint leaves, chiffonade*

A pinch of brown sugar

A splash of rum if you like

½—1 lime, juiced

Salt and pepper

Combine all ingredients in a food processor and pulse twice for a second or two to break it up just a touch.

If you don't have a food processor you can dice everything nice and finely, and then mix thoroughly to combine.

Allow salsa to sit for ten minutes or so before serving so all of the ingredients can get to know each other properly.

Add to chicken, or to some prawns, a piece of pork or even a Christmas ham.

Thank me later.

The French are good for a few things and chopping things in different ways (and making a special word for it) is one of them. Chiffonade is a chopping technique whereby herbs or leafy greens are cut into thin strips.

ROASTED CHICKEN & CHORIZO

WITH CHARRED CHILI PURÉE

(Serves 6)

This is the go-to dish at Chateau le Stockdale, AKA my place, and why wouldn't it be? The combination of chicken and chorizo is the sort of thing that you could put into the Breville sandwich press and it would come out cracking. Put it on a pizza with cow's curd and parsley, in a burger, or in a pasta with cherry tomatoes and mint. On the grill, in the oven, in a pan, as a stew, or on the BBQ are all feasible methods to cook the same ingredients for very different, yet still very similar, results. Brilliant.

6 chicken marylands. Roughly 1½ kg (3½ lb)

2—3 good chorizo sausages, sliced 1 cm thick on the diagonal

1 lemon, quartered

1 onion, cut into wedges

8 cloves of garlic, peeled but left whole

250 ml (8 fl oz) apple cider (for gravy)

2 tbsp plain flour (for gravy)

Salt and pepper

Charred chili puree (recipe 121), to serve

Give the chicken a splash of olive oil, enough so it looks glossy, and then season it with salt and pepper.

Roast at 180°C (350°F) for 30 minutes, then add all other ingredients except apple cider and flour and roast for another 20 or so minutes, until everything is looking golden and tempting.

Once it's all ready, strain the juices into a pan and put on a moderate heat. Mix the flour with a good splash of apple cider to make a slurry. Now whisk the slurry into the pan juices and add the rest of the apple cider. Whisk it all up so it doesn't get lumpy. Cook out for a couple of minutes on a low simmer, adding a little more liquid if it gets too thick.

Check seasoning.

Serve with some tasty sides and the charred chili puree (Page 121).

118

a Cajun classic

Charred Chili Puree

6 fresh jalapeño chilis, charred over an open flame and then peeled

2 cloves garlic, charred and then peeled (it won't be very soft but that's how we want it)

2 tbsp lemon juice or red wine vinegar

120 ml (4 fl oz) olive oil

Combine all ingredients in a suitable container or food processor and blitz.

Check seasoning.

Serve it with chicken or other meats.

Remaining puree will last sealed in the refrigerator for up to 1 week.

PORK CHOP JAMBALAYA

(Serves 4)

Best I can figure, Jambalaya is a bit of a Cajun classic that may have its roots in the Spanish paella. It's a tasty mash up of some kind of meat, smoked sausage, a few vegetables and rice in a pot, where they are left produce immensely good flavor together.

Cajun cooking has a bit of a thing going on with the celery, capsicum (bell pepper) and onion – the holy trinity of Cajun cooking if you will – and it works really well.

Andouille sausage is another ingredient that features a lot in Cajun cooking, but

is a product that I have only recently been able to lay my hands on. So, if you don't know Pastrami Pat, AKA Andouille Pat, chorizo might be the go for you. Here is the recipe for the Pork Chop Jambalaya we ate on one fine evening. It received a standing ovation, which was in fact a sitting 'Yeah, this is really good'. Good enough for me.

4 pork chops

1 Andouille or chorizo sausage, chopped

1 medium brown onion, diced

1 green capsicum (bell pepper), diced

1 stalk celery, diced

5 cloves garlic, minced

1 tbsp Cajun or Creole spice, or even just a pinch of dried thyme and chili

200 g (7 oz) brown rice, soaked in water for a few hours (long grain white rice can also be used, which would not need soaking)

1 L (2 pints) stock or water

Salt and pepper

Chopped parsley, to serve

Heat oil in a heavy-based pan. Season pork chops with salt and pepper and fry in pan until browned on each side but not fully cooked. Set chops aside.

In the same pan, sauté chorizo, vegetables and garlic in rendered pork fat until softened and starting to brown.

Add spice mix and cook out for a further minute.

Add rice, stock and resting pork chops to pan, cover and simmer over low heat for

15–20 minutes or until rice is cooked.

Allow to sit for 5 minutes. Check seasoning.

Garnish with chopped parsley and then serve.

CAMP OVEN CHICKEN

WITH BROAD BEANS & BACON

(Serves 4—6)

It's not hard to eat well while you're camping, it really isn't.

Something as simple as Camp Oven Chicken for example, can be lifted to dizzying new heights if you remember to pack a little ham stock and some broad beans from the garden. It's about the forethought: past Graz looking out for future Graz and all that. I'm certainly not implying that all of your camp meals should be like you're staying at a five-star resort; I can help with your cooking, but I'm not going to provide you with a bath robe and a little mint choccy on your pillow.

1x 1.6 kg (3.5 lb) chicken of prime origin

3 rashers bacon

1 brown onion, diced

1 carrot, diced

1 stick celery, sliced

5 cloves garlic, chopped

3 sprigs fresh thyme or lemon thyme

2–3 cups broad beans, podded (if you can't get them fresh, frozen are readily available and would do the job)

500 ml (16 fl oz) ham stock

Salt and pepper

Sauté bacon, onion, carrot, celery and garlic in a large camp oven* (Dutch oven) until starting to color.

Add your chicken, ham stock and thyme, and season well.

Put the lid on your camp oven and keep it on med-low coals, with a layer of coals on the lid, for 40–50 minutes.

Sweep coals off the lid and check the chook, it should be pretty close. If not, put the lid back on, cover with coals and leave for another 10 minutes. Repeat until ready.

Once the chicken is done, add the broad beans and simmer uncovered for another 10 minutes.

Serve the chicken with bread baked in the camp oven and tune in to the pretty sounds of nature at sunset.

Aaaaaahhhhhhhh.

*All of these camp oven recipes can be cooked in a conventional oven at 180°C (350°F) for similar times.

GREEN PAPAYA SALAD

WITH NAM JIM

(Serves 4—6)

The biggest favour you could do yourself right now is to go to a kitchenware shop and buy yourself a papaya shredder; it looks just like a vegetable peeler, except instead of a flat blade it has corrugations.

1 green papaya

1 continental cucumber, sliced

1 punnet (10—12) cherry tomatoes, sliced in half

2 baby red onions, or half a red onion, sliced finely

A handful of coriander (cilantro), mint and Thai basil. Put your knife through the lot three or four times

2 tbsp crispy eschallots (shallots/ French shallots) (go to the Asian supermarket for these)

2 tbsp crushed peanuts

Nam Jim dressing (recipe on right)

Peel the thick skin off your papaya with a hunky dory vegetable peeler.

Shred your papaya with a julienne shredder or papaya shredder.

Now, in a large mixing bowl, combine the shredded papaya with everything except the crispy shallots and peanuts, and dress generously with Nam Jim.

Put it in a bowl if it's part of a Thai feast, or divide it onto plates as a garnish for your grilled chicken, and sprinkle with crispy shallots and crushed peanuts.

Nam Jim

3 long red chili, deseeded and chopped

1 clove garlic, chopped

3 coriander (cilantro) roots, washed and chopped

3 tbsp shaved light palm sugar

1½ tbsp fish sauce

100 ml (3½ fl oz) lime juice

Combine all ingredients in a blender and blitz until pureed. Alternatively, use a mortar and pestle: place dry ingredients into mortar and pound into a coarse paste, then add wet ingredients and stir to combine.

Store in a sealed container in the refrigerator. Will last for up to 1 week.

BARBECUED CHICKEN

WITH THAI FLAVORS

(Serves 4—6)

1x 1.6 kg (3½ lb) chicken, cut in half down the back bone

½ brown onion, chopped

6 cloves garlic, chopped

1 thumb sized knob galangal, sliced

2 stalks lemongrass, white part only, sliced

3 kaffir lime leaves

2 dried long red chili, more if you like it hot, rehydrated in a little hot water

1 tsp palm sugar (or caster sugar is fine)

1 tbsp fish sauce

Green papaya salad (page 123), to serve

Steamed rice, to serve

Fresh lime, to serve

Crush everything, except the chicken, together with a mortar and pestle or in a food processor. A coarse paste is good.

Rub the paste all over the chicken.

Let that chicken sit in the fridge for at least an hour while you get your fire started. Note: this fire may be your oven if that's all you have. 180°C (350°F) or so should do the trick.

Grill over the quiet part of the fire for

50 minutes or until cooked, turning every 10 minutes or so for smoky, tasty chicken goodness.

Douse with fresh lime juice and serve with a heap of Thai side dishes: start with rice, green papaya salad, pickled cucumber, chili in fish sauce, more chili condiments and whatever else you need.

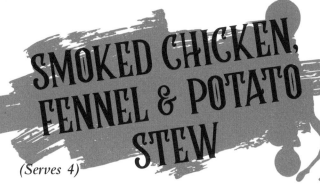

SMOKED CHICKEN, FENNEL & POTATO STEW

(Serves 4)

I had this meal in the pot in 5 minutes, which left me with plenty of time to go out to the veranda and sit back in my old rocking chair, smoking my corncob pipe.

This is a great recipe for lazy, single man. Or, in my world, it's damn tasty and super easy, which leaves me with plenty more time to hide from my screaming children … errr, spend some quality time with my kids.

This is a recipe that will happily use any leftover chicken from the one you smoked last night, frame included, and can be boosted with a bit of smoked pork if you have some in the fridge – I like to keep some in there at all times. It can save your bacon (pun intended) in times of need. It's kind of like keeping Band-Aids in your first aid cabinet. Makes sense, right?

500 g (17½ oz) smoked chicken meat, plus carcass

100 g (3½ oz) smoky pork. Bacon,

SERVE WITH CRUSTY BREAD

Served with mint sauce.

ham or smoked sausage would be the obvious choices, but smoked trotter or hock would also work exceptionally well

2 brown onions, sliced

1 large fennel bulb, sliced

1 stick celery, sliced

1 bunch chard or kale

4 cloves garlic, minced

1 tbsp ground coriander seed

1x 400 g (14 oz) tin of French brown lentils

4 medium potatoes, chopped into large chunks

1 L (2 pints) chicken stock or water

Salt and pepper

Chopped parsley, to garnish

Crusty bread, to serve

Put everything except the lentils, potatoes and chard into a pot and sauté with a good hit of olive oil.

Once things smell appetizing and are starting to color up just a touch, add the potatoes and chicken stock or water (what you might call 'tap stock').

Cover and simmer for 30 minutes or until the potatoes are just about cooked. Remove carcass if using.

Add lentils and simmer for another 5 minutes.

Add chard and simmer for another 5 minutes.

Check seasoning.

Drizzle with a little olive oil.

Serve with big lumps of fresh bread and chopped parsley.

LAMB SCHNITZEL

(Serves 4)

Now, lamb rump is probably so popular because butchers were smart enough to call it something other than what it is. Well played butchers. Well played indeed. But for me, a good, tender lamb rump is something I'm going to be happy to serve up and enjoy.

8x 90–100 g (3–3½ oz) lamb rump steaks, pounded a little bit to flatten

1 tbsp fresh rosemary, chopped

1 tbsp fresh thyme, chopped

Zest of 1 lemon

125 g (4½ oz) plain flour

3 eggs, whisked with a splash of water

200 g (7 oz) panko breadcrumbs

Salt and pepper

Mint sauce (page 128), to serve

Mix the breadcrumbs with the herbs, lemon zest and a pinch of salt and pepper.

Dust the lamb rumps in flour, then egg wash, then breadcrumbs to coat. Do it twice if you want extra crunch.

Shallow fry the schnitzels in medium-hot oil for 1 minute each side.

Drain on absorbent paper for 1 minute.

Serve with mint sauce and whatever sides your mind can conjure up. Or even whack it in a bun for a cracking burger.

MINT SAUCE

125 ml (4 fl oz) apple cider vinegar

50 g (2 oz) caster sugar

A big handful of mint

Salt and pepper

Warm the vinegar and sugar until the sugar is dissolved. Allow to cool.

Add chopped mint leaves, or add them whole and then hit it with a stick whizz.

Season with a little salt and pepper.

That's it.

Tell yourself some things really can be that easy.

ROASTED PORK SHOULDER

WITH PUMPKIN & BROCCOLI & TAHINI-COCONUT DRESSING

This recipe begins with my friend Andrea. He is a man and he is Italian, so it is obvious he would eventually run a wood-fired pizza or pasta restaurant. Andrea opted for the wood-fired pizza business as his career path, mobile to boot, and recently he asked if we would like to look after one of his pizza ovens for a while. Quite frankly I was almost insulted that he thought that was even a question, but I regained my usual composure quickly when he rocked up with pizza oven in tow. It is now parked happily in my backyard with its new friends: the fire pit, spit, bonfire, bullet and offset smoker. What a happy little oven it is now …

Andrea is a friend with benefits.

Anyway, that's where this pork ended up, along with a little roast vegetable number that is a ripper of a salad in its own right. The Tahini Coconut Dressing is also a cracker and you should give it a go even if you think you don't like tahini. You are wrong and you will love it!

For the pork

1 pork shoulder roasted quite simply with a heap of salt and pepper and garlic.

You can find instructions on how to roast a pork shoulder on page 130.

ROASTED PUMPKIN & BROCCOLI SALAD

(Serves 4)

½ small pumpkin, deseeded and diced into large chunks

1 head broccoli, cut into florets

1 bunch of chard or kale, chopped into 3—4 pieces

2 tbsp slivered almonds

2 tbsp pepitas

2 tbsp sunflower seeds

1 tbsp sesame seeds

Tahini-coconut dressing (page 132), to serve

Lube the pumpkin with a little oil and season.

Place in preheated 200°C (400°F) oven for 12 minutes.

Add the broccoli and a splash more oil and continue cooking for another 5 minutes.

When pumpkin is pretty much ready to go add chard or kale and nuts and seeds, and roast for another few minutes or until greens are wilted and nuts are toasty.

Serve with a lump of roasted pork and a good splash of Tahini-Coconut Dressing.

SPICED VEGETABLE & BEAN STEW

WITH EGGS

(Serves 6 but can easily be extended to serve more)

This is the sort of thing I like to cook for camp breakfast (or even when we have a few too many people staying at our house for the weekend).

I like to forage for native fruits and berries, track wild boar and gather eggs for this breakfast feast. Just kidding; in fact I Viking raided everyone's ice boxes and used the pillaged goods to create a communal breakfast. I let my brain be free as it instructed my hands through the motions needed to get this awesome breakfast on the table. I feel my brain worked very well with my hands on this occasion.

This spiced vegetable and bean stew is great with baked eggs, sausages and bacon, and pots of freshly brewed coffee (we are not animals) and tea.

4 big handfuls of diced vegetables such as onion, corn, eggplant (aubergine), capsicum (bell pepper), mushrooms and kale

1 x 400 g (14 oz) tinned cannellini beans

1 x 400 g (14 oz) tinned kidney beans

1 tbsp ground cumin seed

1 tbsp paprika

1 tbsp dried oregano

½ tsp dried thyme

½ tsp dried smoked chili powder

1x 700 ml (1½ pint) bottle of tomato passata

Salt and pepper

6 eggs

Sausages and bacon, to serve

In a large pan over some medium-high heat coals, cook off all of the vegetables except kale with a splash of oil.

Once starting to color and soften add spices and kale and cook out for another couple of minutes.

Add beans, tomato and ½ cup water and simmer, covered, for another 8—10 minutes or until vegetables are cooked. Add another splash of water if it starts to thicken up too much, as you need a wet sauce to poach the eggs in.

Check and adjust the seasoning if necessary.

Make 6 or so little dips in the stew and crack eggs straight into them. Don't be too concerned if they don't stay where you want them to, it will all be good in the end.

Cover the pan and simmer, covered, for another 5 minutes or so (until the eggs are cooked but still a little soft in the middle).

Once cooked, serve with an array of camp fire meats, a pot of coffee, tea, whiskey or whatever it is you drink in the morning, and the company of some nice people.

ROASTED PORK SHOULDER

WITH FENNEL SEED, APPLES & BRUSSELS SPROUTS

(Serves 6, plus plenty of leftovers for lunch the next day or two)

This is something that works for me when my life gets busy; so simple and so damn good. I put it in the oven in the morning when we leave the house and it's ready when we return, hours later. I just need to cook a few sides, open a bottle of wine (or maybe two) and then sit down to a great meal.

1 pork shoulder, 3 kg (6 ½ lb) is plenty for my family

1 tbsp fennel seeds

Salt and pepper

500 g (17½ oz) Brussels sprouts, halved

500g (17½ oz) green apples, quartered and cored

2 brown onions, in large slices

A splash of apple cider vinegar

Put the pork shoulder into a baking dish. Rub it with fennel seeds and a good hit of salt and pepper.

Whack it into the oven at 125°C (250°F) and leave it alone. Go and do some really fun stuff with your family for the day. Seriously, this roast is going to be loving life for a good 5—6 hours.

When you return 5—6 hours later you

can bring the pork out of the oven and admire what it has become.

Place the vegetables in another baking tray. Moisten with a cup of the roasting juices from the pork and the apple cider vinegar, season, whack it in the oven and turn up the heat to 200°C (400°F).

After 15 minutes the vegetables should be close to done. Give them a bit of a toss and send them back to the furnace for another 5 minutes.

Return the pork to the oven too, just to give that crackling a working over. This may take up to 10 minutes but persevere, it will be worth it (if your oven has a top heat/grill/broiler function you can use this to really get the crackle going).

Carve the pork and serve it with the Brussels sprouts and apples, and any other sides you fancy – or even just beer and wine will do the trick.

Tahini-Coconut Dressing

1 cloves garlic

1 tbsp sugar

3 tbsp tahini

1½ tbsp soy sauce (gluten free soy is an option)

100 ml (3½ fl oz) coconut cream

3 tbsp lemon juice

125 ml (4 fl oz) vegetable oil

Salt and pepper

Combine everything except oil in a food processor and blitz for 20–30 seconds.

While the motor is still running, slowly add oil to emulsify.

Pour dressing all over everything because it tastes so damn good.

You like tahini now, eh? You're welcome.

Lasts for 1 week in the refrigerator.

CAMP OVEN LAMB

WITH TOMATO & CANNELLINI BEANS

(Serves 6)

Ah, camping. There's the rolling sound of the ocean licking the shore, birds having a happy time waking you up at 5am, you have the ocean or the river to swim in, a wood fuelled combustion cooking and heating system (AKA the fire), cooking on the aforementioned fire, eating with only the light of a kerosene lantern to illuminate the path from the plate to your mouth, leaving the washing up to the little night creatures that clean your plates while you sleep, the environmentally-friendly composting facilities …

OK. There may be one or two things about camping I'm not so into, but I'm going to let that slide. The food we cook on the fire more than compensates.

It's time for a leg of lamb from the camp oven, with cannellini beans, tomatoes, anchovies and herbs.

1 small lamb shoulder (about 1.5 kg or 3½ lb), bone in for the flavor

1 onion, diced

2 medium carrots, diced

5 cloves garlic, chopped

3 anchovy fillets

2 sprigs rosemary

2 bay leaves

1 tbsp dried oregano

2x 400 g tinned tomatoes

2x 400 g tinned cannellini beans

150 g (5 oz) olives

Salt and pepper

Za'atar (page 20), to serve

Rub the lamb down with the herbs and seasoning.

Put it in the camp oven with onion, carrot, garlic and anchovy, plus ½ cup of water, and cover with lid.

Move a few coals out of the fire and nestle the camp oven into these, then shovel a few more coals on top. Leave it for 2 hours, occasionally turning camp oven and replacing coals.

After 2 hours add tomato and return to the coals for another hour.

Add beans and olives and simmer for another hour or so, or until everything is tender and delicious.

Chop it up or pull it apart the best you can and eat it sprinkled with za'atar, washed down with the finest booze your ice box has to offer.

CAMP OVEN PORK SHOULDER ROAST

WITH VEGETABLES

(Serves 4)

1½ kg (3½ lb) pork shoulder

1 onion, chopped

5 cloves garlic, chopped

3 medium potatoes, chopped into chunks

2 carrots, chopped into chunks

2 capsicum, chopped into chunks

2 tomatoes, chopped into chunks

Salt and pepper

Chimichurri (page 19), to serve

Season the skin of the pork. When you think you have seasoned it enough you should probably season it a little more.

Place pork, onion, garlic and ½ cup water into camp oven resting in medium coals, with a few extra coals on top of the lid, rotating every 30 minutes for 2 ½ hours.

After 2 hours have elapsed, you will need to get your vegetables going. In a second camp oven, douse remaining ingredients in a little oil and nestle into the coals for 30-40 minutes.

By the time they are done the pork should be good to go as well.

Double check pork and vegetables just to be sure and if they're not ready put them back into the coals for another 20 or so minutes.

Once it's all good to go, carve that piece of pork up, get it onto a plate with the vegetables, splash it with some chimichurri and serve.

A very nice piece of pork indeed.

A BIG FAT RUMP STEAK

For everyone to share – as long as it's just my boys and me

(Serves 4)

A big fat grilled steak is a beautiful thing.

1.2 kg (2¾ lb) rump steak in one big piece

A handful of chopped herbs, e.g. thyme, rosemary, parsley

3 cloves garlic, chopped

Salt and pepper

Chimichurri sauce (page19), to serve

Charred corn salsa (following on right), to serve

Potato, carrot and onion salad (following on right), to serve

Lube steak with a splash of olive oil and then rub down with herbs, garlic and seasoning. Allow to marinate in the refrigerator for one hour – bringing onto the bench after 30 minutes to get to room temperature.

Grill over some decent heat until you're happy – keep an eye on it and pull it away from hot spots if it starts to flare up and burn. About 10 minutes either side should be somewhere around medium-rare.

Remove from heat and rest in a warm spot for 10 minutes. Make sure you do rest it – it's a large piece of meat kiddo.

Cut it into big slices across the grain.

Serve with Chimichurri sauce, charred corn salsa, and potato, carrot and onion salad.

Charred Corn Salsa

How do you make charred corn?

OK. Let's take the kernels from 3 cobs of corn and toss them in a hot pan with some oil and half a diced onion until it all has a little bit of color on it. Now put that in a bowl with some fresh herbs – parsley, oregano and coriander (cilantro). Olive oil, lemon or lime juice and seasoning will finish it off nicely.

Potato, Carrot & Onion Salad

Roast the potato, carrot and onion whole in the coals, in foil. Season and dress with olive oil. What could go wrong?

This was one of those times where I wanted to fire up the BBQ but I needed to do something different than the ol' standards.

Enter the meatballs...

Meatballs are absolutely banging when they're cooked in any type of BBQ, and also tasty as when cooked in the oven. The choice is yours. But these meatballs? These meatballs were destined for the kettle BBQ today.

Also, just remember meatballs are so easy to make even a child could do it... so, well, you know... don't be afraid to get your kids to help or even force them to take the whole process and make it their own.

MEATY BALLS

(serves 5 - 6)

500 g beef mince

500 g pork mince

1 onion, peeled and finely diced

2 cloves garlic, crushed

1 cup fresh ricotta, crumbled

¼ cup pinenuts, lightly toasted

¼ cup currants

1 teaspoon ground coriander seed

1 small handful of parsley, chopped

1 sprig rosemary, chopped

1 teaspoon dried oregano

Zest of half a lemon

2 slices sour dough bread, crusts removed, processed into coarse breadcrumbs

A big pinch of salt and pepper

3 cups of your favorite pasta sauce – Dolmio, tomato pasatta, nona's home made special tomato sauce, tinned tomatoes or heinz tomato sauce (depending on your own personal preference and presence of taste buds) – tomato pasatta was my choice

Grated parmesan, to serve

Soft polenta, to serve

Preheat your BBQ or oven to 200 C-ish (390 F).

Saute onion and garlic until softened and just starting to color.

In a large mixing bowl combine all ingredients excpet tomato sauce and mix until amalgamated.

Roll your meatballs*. I rolled mine somewhere in the vicinity of the size of a golf ball.

Pour your sauce of preference into a baking or casserole dish that will fit your balls (heheh).

Place the meatballs into the sauce and then into the BBQ or oven for somewhere between 45 and 60 minutes until cooked through.

Check to see if they are cooked by whatever method you see fit.

Check seasoning in the sauce and adjust if necessary.

Serve on soft polenta with extra sauce, a splash of oilve oil and grated parmesan.

*there is no 'wrong way when it comes to rolling meatballs.

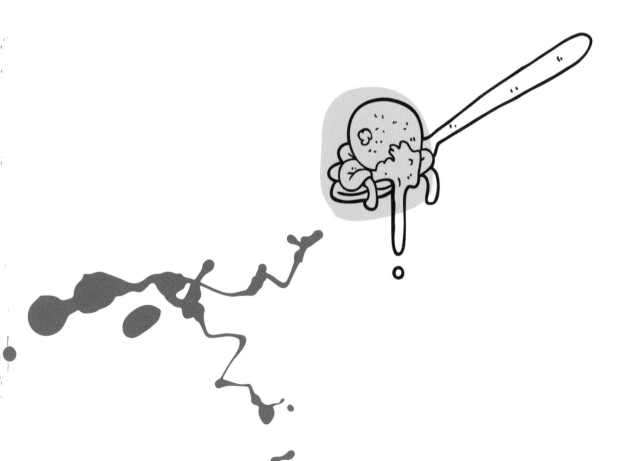

BIG
RED

ABOUT THE AUTHOR

GRAY 'BIG RED' STOCKDALE

I grew up in Albany, Western Australia, the eldest (and smallest at 6 feet 4 inches) of three sons to a hard-working, German-Polish single mum. As the product of hard work, sauerkraut and a distinct lack of flamboyant culinary ability, it is a fucking miracle that I ended up with such an intense passion for everything food has to offer. Miracle or not, I do love it. I live it, I breathe it, and I embody it. I've been called obsessed, neurotic, ridiculous, insane and obscene (all by my wife) with the intensity that I feel for food, but it completely pays off.

Despite my isolated upbringing and sauerkraut-sodden childhood, I now lead a team of renegades into battle every day at my restaurant in Bangalow, New South Wales. From my vantage point in the kitchen, I order, wheedle, cajole and instruct my team, administering light floggings as required. A well olive-oiled machine, we weave our magic to regularly feed 300 people a night on my Southern fried chicken and smokehouse BBQ menu. As is the wont of the kitchen, at the end of the night, we all gather after service to decompress; and I sit back and think to myself 'This over-exploiting,

under-nurturing, catastrophe of a career choice really is the greatest!'

I am fortunate enough to be in the best profession in the world. Sure, the long hours and 50°C (120°F) degree kitchen heat in the middle of summer mean that I may have a severe electrolyte deficiency and a standing prescription for chafe-relief cream every December-through-February. And the constant companionship of people using the vernacular of the sailor means that I will never be able to work in primary schools. But I still reckon it really is the best life ever.

That's what this book is about. It's about how my love for food, and particularly BBQ and fried chicken, has taken over my life. How I gambled everything I had on starting a restaurant, to run it how I wanted to run it, without owners second-guessing my menu and trying to run my ship (I should add, also without their stacks of cash, a definite downside!). It's about how if you believe in something and work hard then it will all work out. And if it doesn't, then I know how to make a damn good meal that I can cry into.

INDEX

First published in 2019 by New Holland Publishers
London • Sydney • Auckland

Bentinck House, 3–8 Bolsover Street, London W1W 6AB, UK
1/66 Gibbes Street, Chatswood, NSW 2067, Australia
5/39 Woodside Ave, Northcote, Auckland 0627, New Zealand

newhollandpublishers.com

A record of this book is held at the British Library and the National Library of Australia.

ISBN 9781760790240

Group Managing Director: Fiona Schultz
Publisher: Fiona Schultz
Project Editor: Elise James
Designer: Yolanda La Gorcé
Food Photography: Rebecca Elliott
Production Director: Arlene Gippert
Printer: Toppan Leefung Printing Limited

10 9 8 7 6 5 4 3 2 1

Keep up with New Holland Publishers on Facebook
facebook.com/NewHollandPublishers